The Collector's Encyclopedia of
LIMOGES PORCELAIN

Second Edition

by Mary Frank Gaston

COLLECTOR BOOKS

A Division of Schroeder Publishing Co., Inc.

TO JERRY AND JEREMY

The current values in this book should be used only as a guide. They are not intended to set prices, which vary from one section of the country to another. Auction prices as well as dealer prices vary greatly and are affected by condition as well as demand. Neither the Author nor the Publisher assumes responsibility for any losses that might be incurred as a result of consulting this guide.

Contents

Acknowledgments

I would like to express my appreciation to several individuals who were instrumental to this second edition. First, I thank my publisher, Bill Schroeder, for seeing the need for this additional survey of Limoges porcelain and publishing this, my twelfth book, for Collector Books. I also thank my editor, Steve Quertermous, who has always been so helpful in assisting me on all of my projects. He is a very busy person, but he always takes the time to answer all questions and see that the rough copy and photographs result in a beautiful book.

Several collectors are responsible for the photographs featured in this edition. I am certainly indebted to Quentin "Reed" Welty of Wooster, Ohio, who has a very extensive collection of Limoges. Jerry and I had the pleasure of visiting with him and his wife, Gloria, a few years ago. We were not able at that time to photograph as much as I needed, and Quentin photographed numerous examples and sent them to me. His help has been immeasurable.

Lota Smith of Dallas, Texas, is an advanced collector of Haviland china. She permitted us to photograph from her large collection which also included pieces by Charles Field Haviland and his successors, GDM, and GDA. Lota was so helpful in providing catalogs documenting certain items and sharing her information and expertise on the subject. Thanks so much.

I also thank Diane and Maurice McGee of Fort Payne, Alabama, who sent many photographs of pieces from their Limoges collection. Other contributors include:

HelenLu Anderson
Patricia and Ludy Benjamin, Bryan, Texas
Rick Brown, Farmington Hills, Michigan
Lewis Brown

Betty E. Bryner, Umatilla, Florida
Lorraine Caffall, Texas City, Texas
Rae Choma, West Bloomfield, Michigan
Muriel Davis
Mrs. Grace B. Franklin, Atascadero, California
Pam Haisty
Claire Hohnstein
Iva Johnson
Mary and Lance Loring
Dorothy Megee
Susan S. Olsson, Chicago, Illinois
Richard Paroutaud, Chehalis, Washington
River Oaks Antique Center, Houston, Texas
Edward S. Rutowski, Erie, Pennsylvania
Audrey and Dan Shanahan, Southern California
Charlene S. Smith, Shelton, Washington
Marie Stine
Glenn and Sue Tingley, Seafaire Antiques, Lincoln City, Oregon
Marceline White
Marian Zickefoose

Finally, I thank my husband, Jerry, for photographing many of the pieces for this book and for his unending patience, help, and interest over the last ten years while I have pursued this hobby and avocation of writing about collectible china.

Pieces featured on the cover are from the Welty collection.

Preface

When I became an antiques dealer several years ago, I specialized in porcelain dinner services. These sets were manufactured by various companies in America, England, France, Czechoslovakia, and Germany. In the course of acquiring these services, I found many with "Limoges" stamped on the back, combined with, or incorporated within marks and initials which I did not recognize. I knew, however, that they were not the marks of the well-known Haviland Company which had been established in Limoges, France, during the mid 1800s. I was familiar with the marks of the Haviland Company because good reference materials are available, not only for the marks of the company but also for the history, prices, and even patterns of that firm. However, I had a difficult time documenting the other Limoges marks, and often I could not.

As time passed, and I gained experience through attending and exhibiting at antiques shows, I discovered many other objects that carried Limoges marks. Most of these pieces were beautifully decorated and often hand-painted. Examples included both large and ornate objects such as vases, jardinieres, and tankards as well as small decorative pieces such as trinket boxes, inkwells, and individual candle holders. The beauty, craftsmanship, and artwork, in addition to the variety of objects, fascinated me. I soon discovered that I was not alone in my appreciation of this porcelain. Dealers and collectors considered Limoges porcelain as a definite category of antiques.

I began buying examples of handpainted Limoges for resale in addition to dinnerware and table items. I was pleased to find that such objects sold well. As my interest in "Limoges" marked objects increased, I wanted to find out more about the individual items. Very little information was available either from books of marks, history sources, or general antiques reference books. The information that was available was widely scattered (and, as I have learned since, much was incorrect). Some sources would have information about one company; but the same facts might be missing from another source which might have information about marks or companies not included in the first source. Sometimes the information was conflicting. In order to find marks, I often had to find "Limoges" in the index and then proceed to look up each page listed under that name. Price guides often included a Limoges section, but the information rarely included the name of the company of manufacture. Usually items were just described according to size and style of decoration with no company name or mark attributed to them.

From other antiques dealers I discovered that even though they might have beautiful examples of Limoges porcelain for sale, they did not always know about the history of the articles, except that they were French. Knowledge was scant concerning the marks on the items. Some might say "This is D and C Limoges." or "This is T and V Limoges." But who or what was "D and C?" or "T and V?" Did these initials stand for a specific company? Did one company use one or several combinations of initials? What did two or three different marks mean on an article? How old was the piece? Such specific questions were often answered with "Well, all I know is that this (object) is Limoges." It seemed then that the name, *Limoges*, spoke for the porcelain. The eye can see the beauty and craftsmanship of the piece. Knowledgeable dealers and collectors can tell by the feel, shape, type, and decoration of an article that the object was not made yesterday, that it is indeed old enough to warrant being collectable. The lack of knowledge concerning who had made the piece or when it had been made did not detract from the price.

Items that are marked, beautifully decorated, and are examples of quality porcelain command good prices. During my searches through shops and at shows I found that prices varied. The smaller shops which did not specialize particularly in china sometimes had pieces priced quite low. Occasionally there was a "steal" at a flea market. But from traveling through various parts of the country, I find that each year the "steals" are increasingly harder to find. This indicates that there is a good market for Limoges porcelain, and that serious collectors need a source of information.

Whether we are collectors of antique china or merely buying an antique as a decorative accessory or a gift, we like to know as much as possible about what we are buying. We want to know where it came from, who made it, and what it was used for, if this is not obvious.

My purpose in this book is to provide, all in one source, information on the history, marks, products, and current market prices for the porcelain manufactured and exported by companies in Limoges during the mid to late nineteenth century through the first third of the twentieth century, circa the 1930s or prior to World War II. From the beginning of porcelain manufacturing in Limoges in the late 1700s until the 1930s, there have been literally hundreds of names (factories, decorators, exporters) connected with the industry. It would be an impossible task to document every name connected with the industry during this period.

This book primarily reflects the Limoges items which

are currently available on the American antiques market, most of which date from the late 1860s to the 1930s. Most of the very old Limoges wares prior to the mid-1800s are in museums. A few of the older names and marks are included for reference purposes, as are some companies which did not carry on an extensive export trade with the United States but are well known in Europe. Some of the names listed in the first edition, however, have been deleted because no examples have surfaced, and it is apparent that their production was not geared to export to the United States. I also have not included some names connected with the Limoges porcelain industry which may be found in other reference books because those companies originated after 1930, the arbitrary cut-off date for most of the material included in this book.

My first book on Limoges porcelain was published in 1980, and in 1984, the book was reprinted with revised prices, including a method of "ranking" examples according to French or American decoration. I am very pleased to have this second edition published by Collector Books. This new edition contains five hundred color photographs, the majority being pieces not shown in the first book. A very few pictures have been reprinted from the first edition in order to show an example of a particular company for which a new piece was not available or to include an example of a rare object or exquisite decoration.

Please note that the David Haviland Company and Theodore Haviland Company are included in this book. These companies were not part of the first book, and in 1984, my book *Haviland Collectables and Objects of Art* was published by Collector Books. At this time, however, it seems appropriate to include these Haviland companies to make this study on Limoges more complete. Marks have been reprinted from the Haviland book, but the reader should refer to that book for more detailed historical information on the company and for different photographs of examples of their production.

Some American and European publications supplied helpful information and enabled me to start piecing together the puzzle of Limoges porcelain while I was writing the first edition. After my book had gone to press, a superb reference, in French, was released: *La Porcelaine de Limoges* by Jean d'Albis and Céleste Romanet. If that book had been published earlier, many of the conflicting points about various companies would have been clarified. I do thank the authors for answering some of my questions when I wrote to them before their book was released. Their book is footnoted in this edition for information concerning several of the companies and marks. Please see all of these entries in the Bibliography for further and detailed study of the subject of Limoges porcelain.

I hope that this book will make it easier for the beginner as well as the advanced collector, dealer, and appraiser to identify, document, and price examples of Limoges porcelain. I look forward to continuing my study of Limoges by documenting marks and objects not covered in this revised work. Readers who have examples with Limoges marks which are not included may write to me at the address listed below. Please include a self-addressed stamped envelope if a reply is requested.

Mary Frank Gaston
P.O. Box 342
Bryan, TX 77806-0342

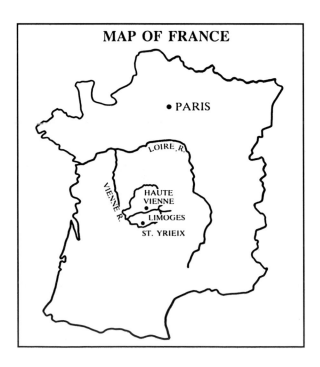

MAP OF FRANCE

The Unique Quality of Porcelain

Porcelain is pottery in its most exquisite form. The word "porcelain" comes from the Portuguese word "porcella," the name for the shell made by a type of mollusk, the cowrie. This shell is translucent, and the Portuguese gave this name to the translucent pottery they were importing from China during the 1500s. To understand the unique quality of porcelain, translucency, it is necessary to understand the processes that each type of pottery requires for production. A brief summary here of these processes will give a basic understanding of the differences among the types of pottery. (Some references in the Bibliography give detailed descriptions.)

Pottery is any object made of clay and fired (or baked) at a high temperature. Clay is a form of earth. Earth, depending on its location, is composed of different natural ingredients. Thus the type of pottery which can be made in an area is determined by the presence and type of ingredients found in the earth in that area.

There are two types of pottery: earthenware and stoneware. Pottery is "earthenware" if it has a porosity of more than 5 percent. Earthenware articles may be waterproof if they are covered by a glaze, but the glaze and the body of the object are not fused together during the firing process. As a result, the glaze of earthenware can be penetrated. And, if the glaze is penetrated, crazing usually results. Crazing is tiny hairlines that develop under the glaze on the surface of the object. Crazing detracts from the appearance of the article and weakens it. Also if the glaze is penetrated, certain liquids which might come in contact with the surface of the object can cause staining or discoloration. Earthenware is not as durable as stoneware. Earthenware can be made from many different types of natural clays including kaolin, ball clay, and cornish stone. Earthenware is fired at temperatures below 1200 degrees centigrade which is lower than the temperature at which stoneware is fired. If a glaze is applied to the object, it is refired below 1100 degrees centigrade. Earthenware is opaque and may be glazed like majolica or remain unglazed like clay flower pots.

Pottery is "stoneware" if it has a porosity of less than 5 percent. Stoneware is fired at extremely high temperatures, 1200 to 1400 degrees centigrade. During the first firing, the body and glaze melt or fuse together and become vitrified, that is, like glass. This vitreous quality results in the low percentage of porosity. Stoneware can have but need not have additional glazes applied after the first firing, because the vitreous quality is achieved during the first firing. Stoneware is made from natural stoneware clays which are of a sedimentary type and fine grained. These clays are quite plastic, meaning that they can be worked with and shaped easily. Stoneware is opaque. Stoneware items are heavier than earthenware items. They are also harder and more durable. Basalt, ironstone, and certain types of crockery are examples of stoneware.

Technically, porcelain is considered to be a special type of stoneware. The reason for this is that porcelain, like stoneware, is fired to a state of vitrification. However stoneware is not fired to a state of translucency as porcelain is. Porcelain objects are first fired at a temperature of around 900 degrees centigrade. A glaze is then applied, and the article refired at from 1300 to 1500 degrees centigrade. Vitreosity is attained during this second firing. Although porcelain is vitreous, like stoneware, it is also translucent whereas other stoneware is opaque. Translucent means that light can pass through an object. Opaque means that light cannot pass through an object. Put your hand behind a plate, a cup, a bowl, or the bottom of a figurine and hold it up to the light. If it is porcelain, you will be able to see the shadow of your hand through the object. The better you can see the shadow, the thinner the porcelain. This translucent quality of porcelain is obtained from the type of ingredients used in the paste. Paste is the basic clay and other minerals which are mixed together to form a particular object.

After the object formed from the paste is fired for the first time, the resulting product is called bisque or biscuit, meaning unglazed. The bisque is translucent at this stage, but it is not vitreous. To achieve vitreosity the object must be baked a second time with a glaze. It is during this second firing that the glaze and body melt together resulting in a glass-like product. Articles can be decorated before or after the glaze is applied and the article baked the second time. More than one glaze and different colored glazes can be used.

Porcelain is whitish in color in its natural state before the glazes have been applied. If an object is not glazed and remains in the bisque form, it has a higher degree of porosity. Figurines are examples of porcelain which are often found in bisque. The base of some glazed wares may be left in bisque form to allow the object to grip a surface better. Glazed porcelain is slick like glass, so articles such as vases, dresser boxes, and trays are not as likely to slide on a surface if their base is unglazed. Some erroneously think that the object is not well made or not finished if the base is left as bisque.

The distinguishing characteristic of porcelain as compared to earthenware and other forms of stoneware is its translucency. Because of this difference, many prefer to divide pottery into three categories: earthenware, stoneware, and porcelain. The three classifications do seem more helpful for ease in identification.

Other differences between porcelain and earthenware and stoneware are that porcelain objects are not as heavy as stoneware and have a more delicate appearance. Earthenwares can be light in weight like porcelain, but they are not as strong. Porcelain will not craze as earthenware does. Porcelain objects may break or develop a crack if some force is applied. The break line will just appear where the force was applied, but the other parts of the surface will not develop lines or crazing. Porcelain is nonporous whereas earthenware is porous under the glaze. If the glaze of an earthenware object is penetrated, matter can become "trapped" under the glaze. Porcelain glazes cannot be penetrated. If some harmful substance comes into contact with the surface of porcelain, it can be washed off. The object will not be discolored or stained. Earthenware can be produced more cheaply than porcelain because it is fired at lower temperatures. The natural ingredients necessary to make both earthenware and stoneware exist in many areas throughout the world, but there are comparatively few areas in the world with deposits of the natural ingredients needed to make porcelain.

Porcelain is divided into three types: bone paste, soft paste, and hard paste. The paste type depends on the type and percentage of basic ingredients used as well as the process of manufacture. All three types are translucent in both the bisque and glazed states, they are light in weight but still strong, and they are vitreous if glazed.

Bone paste (or bone china) is so called because its principal ingredient is an ash made from calcined animal bone. This bone ash constitutes at least 50% of the paste with such materials as china clay and feldspar making up the rest of the formula. The paste is not as white in color as that of hard paste. Bone paste is stronger than soft paste porcelain, and the manufacturing process is cheaper than that of soft paste. Bone paste is fired at a lower temperature than hard paste. The product is first fired unglazed to a translucent state at a temperature of over 1200 degrees centigrade. It is fired a second time with the glaze at a lower temperature, below 1100 degrees centigrade. The Spode, Worcester, and Wedgwood factories introduced bone china in England during the latter part of the 1700s and early 1800s. England is still the center for this type of porcelain production.

Soft paste porcelain is known as *pâte tendre* or *petit feu* in French. The latter term refers to the degree of temperature needed for the firing process which is lower than those required for bone paste and hard paste. The porcelain is not actually "soft." Objects are first fired at about 1100 degrees centigrade and at a lower temperature with the glaze at the second firing. Due to the lower firing temperatures, this type of porcelain is not as durable as bone paste or hard paste. The glazes can be scratched, and there is thus some degree of porosity under the glaze.

Europeans long admired the hard paste porcelain products of China, but they did not know the formula for this type of manufacture. During the 1600s, primarily in France, soft paste production was begun as an attempt to imitate the hard paste Chinese porcelain. Soft paste was actually an artificial type of porcelain in those days. Glass or glass like materials were ground up and mixed with clay and other ingredients. This glass matter was known as the frit and was necessary to cause the other materials in the paste to melt together and achieve the translucent and vitreous qualities. Lead was also used in the glazes to enable easier fusing of the glaze and the body. In the early days of soft paste production, the clay and glassy materials were often not well mixed, and the firing process was not evenly controlled. As a result some parts of an object were more translucent than other parts. Chemical analysis was not very sophisticated so often the proportion of ingredients varied resulting in uneven quality products. Sometimes the pieces became warped and developed cracks during the firing. Many pieces of soft paste were wasted due to the inexact manufacturing process. Although the soft paste process is still costly today, the formulas can be exact and the firing process controlled. Also the natural ingredient feldspar is used instead of bits of glass to achieve translucency and vitreosity. Lead, which is harmful for table china, does not have to be used in the glazes.

Hard paste porcelain is known as *pâte duré* or *grand feu* in French, meaning that such porcelain is fired at very high temperatures. Hard paste is considered to be a natural porcelain because its ingredients exist in the earth. This is not the case with bone china, or the seventeenth and eighteenth century soft paste mixtures. Kaolin and feldspar are the principal ingredients for hard paste porcelain. Kaolin which accounts for about 50% of the paste is a type of earth containing hydrated aluminum silicates. The word comes from the Chinese "Kao-ling," the name of the mountain region in China where this type of earth was found many centuries ago. Feldspar or petuntze (petuntse) is the other important natural ingredient. Feldspar comes from a rock, and it is necessary both in the paste and the glaze. Feldspar adds strength to the paste allowing the object to be fired at a high temperature and to become translucent. The glaze and object are made of similar materials, but the glaze contains a larger percentage both of feldspar and quartz enabling the glaze and paste object to melt together and fuse into one entity. The object is then vitreous or like glass. Hard paste objects are first fired at around 900 degrees centigrade. The second firing with the glaze is from 1400 to 1600 degrees centigrade.

The secret of making hard paste was not known in Europe until circa 1708. Johann Friedrich Böttger, an alchemist, of Meissen (Germany) is credited with this discovery which led a few years later to the establishment of a hard paste factory in Meissen (the Meissen factory) and thus the first of its kind in Europe. Once the formula for "true" or "natural" porcelain was known, many of the problems and guesswork connected with earlier soft paste production were eliminated. When the natural ingredients of kaolin and feldspar were discovered in other regions, the potters of those areas were eager to turn to making hard paste porcelain.

The Story of Limoges Porcelain

Limoges porcelain is hard paste porcelain. Limoges is the city where factories producing this type of porcelain have been located for a little over 200 years. The name of the city has in fact become synonymous with the high quality porcelain products manufactured by those companies. Tilmans (page 217), a French writer, put it aptly:

> Le Limousine semble prédestiné
> á abriter les Arts du Feu.

That means literally that the Limousine region of France seemed predestined to be the home for the arts of fire (porcelain). Why? Because the soil of the area surrounding Limoges is rich in deposits of kaolin and feldspar, the essential ingredients for natural, or hard paste, porcelain. Equally important is the fact that pottery making, particularly faience, was carried on in the area prior to the discovery of kaolin. Thus the people with the special knowledge, skills, and equipment were available and ready to start hard paste production when the formula was known and the necessary ingredients were discovered in the area. Additionally of importance, when porcelain first began to be produced in Limoges during the late 1700s, the region had plentiful forests to supply the necessary fuel for the kilns, and the rivers provided easy transportation facilities for the wood.

The city of Limoges is located about 200 miles south of Paris in the region known as the Haute Vienne. The Vienne is the principal river flowing through the area. The town itself is located at the base of the mountain Mont Jovis. Kaolin was discovered near Limoges at the village of Saint Yrieix in 1768. The discovery of this essential ingredient for hard paste porcelain is attributed to Mme. Darnet, the wife of a local doctor. Tests made of the white earth she found proved it in fact to be a pure and superior form of kaolin.

The discovery of this clay near Limoges did not occur, however, until about 60 years after the formula for making hard paste porcelain had been discovered by Böttger of Meissen. Although the Meissen company had tried to keep the formula a secret, the knowledge eventually spread to other areas in Europe as workers left the company and took the knowledge of the process with them. Of course the knowledge was useless if the necessary ingredients for porcelain were not available. The advantages of hard paste over the artificial, or soft paste, porcelain were well known by the time kaolin was discovered at Saint Yrieix. Possession of both the formula and the basic ingredient in that area naturally led to experiments in the production of hard paste porcelain. The Royal Court of France recognized the importance of the kaolin discovery, and Turgot, in charge of Finance for King Louis XVI, thought it advantageous to help the industry to get started in France.

The first production of hard paste porcelain at Limoges is attributed to the company of Massie, Grellet, and Fourneira. Massie was the owner of a faience factory which had been established by his father near Limoges in 1737. Following the discovery of kaolin in the area, Massie, circa 1770, became partners with brothers by the name of Grellet, and a chemist by the name of Fourneira. Experiments were begun by the company in making hard paste porcelain. The company was granted the permission to make this form of porcelain products by an order of the Council of the Court. In 1777 the company came under the patronage of the Comte d'Artois, brother of King Louis XVI. Patronage, in effect, meant that the company was financed and supported by the Count. The products were required to be marked with the initials "C.D." These initials were written in various forms, sometimes with the coat of arms of the Count, in different colors, or incised into the porcelain. Pieces carrying these marks are in museums today. (I have not included these marks in this book because they do not represent useful information about porcelain available on the market today. For more information on these marks see sources in the Bibliography.)

The company encountered problems, both financial and technical, during the first years of operation. The owners as early as 1774 had tried to sell the factory to the King. The sale did not take place though until ten years later, in 1784. In the meantime progress was made in hard paste production. When the firm was taken over by the King, however, it was neither allowed to carry on the type of production it had started nor to remain a separate company. Louis XVI used the factory as a branch of Sèvres, the Royal Porcelain Company that manufactured soft paste porcelain. White wares were made at Limoges and then sent to Sèvres for decoration. Thus many Sèvres pieces during this time were in fact Limoges porcelain. One of the original founders of the Limoges company, the younger Grellet brother, directed the factory after it was taken over by the king. He served as manager from 1784 until 1788. Markings on the Limoges products during this time included the word "royalle." J. François Alluaud succeeded Grellet as manager of the royal Limoges company. He served from 1788 until 1794. The French *fleur de lys* symbol was used as a mark during this period. The operations of the company were interrupted by the French Revolution. Circa 1794 the factory was sold to three of the workers:

Joubert, Cacate, and Joly.

The end of the Revolution circa 1796 allowed the porcelain industry of the Limousine region to progress. Another hard paste company had been established as early as 1774 near Saint Yrieix by the Comte de la Seynie, evidence that interest in this type of production was not confined to the Massie and Grellet company. Following the Revolution there was no monopoly in the business, and other companies were formed at Limoges. Alluaud, former director of the Royal Limoges Company, set up a factory of his own circa 1798. Monnerie and Baignol are other names associated with the Limoges industry at the end of the eigthteenth century.

The beginning years of the nineteenth century witnessed greater expansion. It is noted that the industry employed approximately 200 workers circa 1807 but by 1830 the number had increased to over 1,800. The period of the mid to late 1800s was actually the golden age for the Limoges porcelain industry. Production became industrialized. New methods of manufacture and decoration were introduced. The companies were able to benefit from mass production techniques. This was important in order to meet the growing demand of a large export market. During this period approximately 75% of the porcelain manufactured in the area was exported. The largest market was American, but the people of other European countries also wanted examples of this fine quality porcelain. The number of companies increased from around 32 during the mid to late 1800s, to 48 in the 1920s. The porcelain industry was the chief employer of the people of the Limoges area. Men were not the only ones employed; in fact whole families often worked for the companies. The numerous processes necessary to bring off a finished piece of porcelain required many hands from the manufacturing of the products down to the shipping of the goods for export. There were many jobs that could be done by women and children.

In America, and also Canada, Limoges table china, especially that made by the Haviland Company, became a status symbol for brides. Art objects and decorative accessories made by the Limoges companies were also in demand by the American consumer. These porcelain items were not cheap for the times, but that did not lessen the demand. Limoges porcelain was prized due to the exquisite quality and beautiful decoration of the pieces. America was in the full swing of a historical era typified by an extremely elaborate life style. Victoriana dictated the tastes of the period. Many different and unusual items were considered not only proper but necessary for the decoration of home and table, not only for the very wealthy but also for those of more modest means. The living and social customs portrayed by books and pictures of that bygone era seem quite lavish when compared to today's standards.

The Limoges manufacturers were happy to take advantage of the wants and whims of the American market. They soon were catering to the American market in the types of objects produced. American table customs and tastes differed somewhat from those of the French, thus many products were made and decorated especially for the American market.

In the early years of the 1900s, however, a crisis developed in the industry. The companies were producing more porcelain than the market could absorb. Many of the older companies were forced out of business, unable to compete with the younger companies. The newer firms were able to adapt to new ideas, and they had more capital resources necessary for the large scale production of porcelain. The first World War circa 1914 followed by the world wide economic crises of the late 1920s and 1930s brought about the end of the prosperity of the porcelain industry in Limoges. It was some years after the second World War before the industry was able to be revitalized. The introduction of gas to the factories in the late 1940s enabled more modern, efficient, and less expensive methods of production. Today Limoges is still the center of hard paste porcelain production in France. The quality of the wares is still superb.

However, the porcelain produced in Limoges from the mid 1800s until approximately 1930 is the porcelain that is of interest to antiques collectors. It is the examples from this period that are currently seen on the American antiques market. The year 1930 is of course an arbitrary cut-off date. One of the reasons for this is the age factor. Porcelain made at Limoges before 1930 is from 50 to over 100 years old. The date also reflects the end of an era. The stock market crash of 1929 and the depression of the 1930s brought an end to the life style prior to that time. Undoubtedly the porcelain produced by Limoges factories after 1930 too will be collected by future generations for quality is always recognized.

Comparing Haviland and Other Limoges Porcelain

Although hard paste porcelain production actually began as early as 1773 in Limoges, France, with numerous companies operating there since the early 1800s, there is really only one company by name that is immediately recognized today, especially in the United States: Haviland and Company. The Haviland factory actually began producing porcelain in Limoges in 1865 (d'Albis and Romanet, p. 134). At that time, hard paste porcelain production had been in progress at Limoges for roughly 90 years.

The porcelain factories which were established at Limoges before and after the Haviland company were primarily French owned and operated. Prior to the the mid 1800s their products were made for the European market. It was only after 1840 that the companies attempted any large scale exportation of their products to the United States. Many of these companies were small, and some were in business for only a short time. Other firms either changed management, consolidated with, or became absorbed by other companies at various points in time. Records of the companies were often not well kept or became lost through the years. As a result, our knowledge about them is not complete.

Why, then, is the Haviland Company so much better known than the other companies? Prior to locating in France, David Haviland had owned and operated a business in New York for importing china, primarily English earthenwares. In order to improve business during the late 1830s, David Haviland and his brother, Daniel, imported some French porcelain. Americans did not find the dishes appealing. They did not object to the dishes being French porcelain rather than English earthenware, but they did not like the decoration, and sets included pieces which they were not accustomed to using.

Obviously realizing that hard paste porcelain was superior to earthenware, Haviland sought to solve the objections of his customers. He first traveled to France in 1840 and later settled in Limoges about 1842. During the first several years there, he selected porcelain made by other Limoges companies and exported the wares to his New York firm. He eventually opened his own decorating studio where his artists decorated china made by other Limoges factories. Finally, some twenty-five years after he had moved to Limoges, Haviland began producing china. His products, primarily dinner services, were designed almost exclusively for the American market. Americans enthusiastically bought these lovely products. The American demand for the china increased at a high rate. Haviland china was sold in stores and through catalog

ordering houses. The Jewel Tea Company, a large grocery firm, offered Haviland china as premiums when people purchased Jewel products. In that way many people who might not have been able to buy a set outright collected an entire dinner service over a period of time. These services were greatly prized and handed down to future generations.

The Haviland company gained fame not only in America, but most importantly also in France. David Haviland is considered partly responsible for the turning point of the Limoges porcelain industry that occurred during the mid 1800s. He was instrumental in creating a large demand for Limoges porcelain on the American market which in turn benefited the other companies. Americans liked Limoges products, and the people did not think that the ware necessarily had to be manufactured by the Haviland firm. Large department stores in the United States requested other companies as well as Haviland to make porcelain items especially for them. Marks for these stores are often seen as additional marks on pieces of Limoges porcelain. (See the marks descriptions in the photographic section.)

Not only did David Haviland aid in opening up the American market for Limoges porcelain, but he also introduced new methods of technology for production and decoration which were superior to those previously used. He was responsible also for changing the practice of the companies of sending their white wares out of the factory to other studios for decoration. He made the decorating workshops part of his factory thus saving time and money, marks of an efficient American businessman! Eventually other companies followed this procedure. Innovative and time-saving techniques were necessary at this period in the history of the industry in order to meet the growing export demand. Those factories which were able to emulate Haviland's techniques, and in effect, compete with the Haviland company, were able to reap the benefits of the American trade. The other companies were in fact anxious to take advantage of this market. Evidence of this is seen by the quantity and various types of articles carrying the marks of so many different Limoges companies which are seen today on the American antiques market.

The porcelain objects which we see today that were manufactured by the Haviland company or by other china companies in Limoges from the mid 1800s to the early 1900s are examples of hard paste porcelain. (Note that Haviland and some of the other companies did make soft paste and faience, but the hard paste wares are the ones typically identified with the name "Limoges" and those companies.) The basic ingredients used by all of the companies to make the porcelain came from the same area, the Limousine region of France. The methods and specific techniques of manufacture of course varied through time and from company to company. The basic differences between Haviland porcelain and the porcelain made by other Limoges companies are not in the quality of the porcelain, but in the types of articles manufactured and the type of decorating employed. The Haviland company primarily produced dinner services, in thousands of different patterns, for the American market. The patterns of the china were characterized by transfer decoration of delicate floral designs. It is this image that comes to mind when one says "Haviland." The other companies also manufactured dinner services, but in lesser quantity than the Haviland company. Usually their designs and colors were much bolder than Haviland's. But dinner services are not the most representative items that we see for these other companies. Their products include a wide range of objects broadly classified as decorative accessories. (See the section on decorative accessories for the specific types of articles.) These pieces were most often vividly decorated, and frequently handpainted, with floral, fruit, figural, and scenic themes. Pieces were often elaborately fashioned and embellished with gold. The combination of the ornate golden trim with the deep and vibrant colored designs gives the objects a very rich appearance. It is this image that comes to mind when one says "Limoges."

This, of course, is not to say that the Haviland company did not produce decorative accessories and art objects ornately fashioned and richly decorated, or that the other companies did not manufacture dinner services with delicate designs. The difference is in the emphasis on such items. One sees more "Limoges" decorative accessories and art objects than Haviland art objects; likewise one sees more Haviland dinner ware patterns than "Limoges" dinner ware patterns.

Both Haviland and other Limoges companies exported large amounts of undecorated porcelain to the United States. This unpainted porcelain was referred to as white wares or blanks. These pieces were available in almost any type of object that was thought necessary at the time to enhance home and table decoration. Individuals and decorating firms purchased this white ware. China painting was popular during this period of history. Special schools were established to teach that particular art form, and some people even had their own kilns. China painting during this period is often portrayed as the work of women, but one sees many fine examples signed with men's names. These handpainted white wares are in demand and collected today as well as pieces decorated in France at Limoges. It is interesting to note that the style of decoration typical of the "Limoges" image is also reflected in the American decoration of these white ware items. This was probably an attempt to emulate the Limoges decorative style as well as the preferred artistic tastes of the mid to late Victorian period. Again one sees more white ware items, decorated in this country, with the mark of some other Limoges company than Haviland, another indication of the trend of the exporting practices of the companies.

A large quantity of porcelain made by the Haviland company and the many other Limoges companies during the peak of the industry, from the middle 1800s to the first quarter of the 1900s, is available in the United States today. These porcelain objects, factory decorated or studio and individually decorated, are considered collector's items.

Because of the good records maintained by the Haviland company one is able, through various reference sources, to identify the different marks used by the company and the dates when the marks were in use. Books identify many of the patterns of Haviland china made during this time. Haviland matching services exist throughout the United States. In the following pages, the reader should be able to learn more about the many other Limoges companies and see from the color photographs the fine and varied porcelain objects made by these firms. (For a more detailed discussion of David Haviland and illustrations of Haviland basically contrary to the "Haviland image," see my book *Haviland Collectables and Objects of Art*, 1984).

Identifying Limoges Porcelain

Objects are prized because of their unique qualities. Some types of objects appeal to some people and different types of objects appeal to others—it is a matter of individual taste. We can like or collect certain items because they appeal to us, but the more we know about the items, the more our appreciation is enhanced. Also from a pragmatic view, many people collect certain objects as a form of investment, so facts become important to insure that such investments are worthwhile.

Information is always gained through study and experience. For Limoges porcelain collectors, it is important to become familiar with the historical period that represents the time when those items which are considered collector's items today were being manufactured. The social customs and artistic tastes of the period influenced the type of items made and the style of decoration. Visiting antiques shops and antiques shows enables one to see the examples of the various firms. In this way one can examine the objects closely and become familiar with the types of items and styles of decoration firsthand. It is also wise to visit gift shops and department stores to compare modern porcelain pieces with those of the earlier period. Through such experiences one becomes able to differentiate more easily between late and early products.

Types of Wares

In discussing the products of the various Limoges companies, the types of objects have been broadly grouped into three categories for simplification.
(1) The category *art objects* includes large objects such as vases; decorative plaques; tankards; mugs; trays; decorative bowls and plates; paintings; jardinieres.
(2) The category *decorative accessories* includes small items such as dresser sets; trinket boxes; candleholders; cachepots; baskets, receiving card trays; small vases; tobacco jars, inkwells, stamp boxes.
(3) The category *table china* includes berry, pudding, and ice cream sets; cake plates; compotes; coffee and demi-tasse sets; chocolate sets; teapots; cider pitchers; juice pitchers; decorative creamers and sugars; cracker jars; jam jars; pancake dishes; punch bowls; fish and game services. The majority of these pieces are hand decorated entirely or partially. Also included in the category of table china are place settings and serving pieces for dinner services representing different patterns manufactured by Limoges companies. Many items classified as table china would also be considered as art objects, especially the game and fish services and other handpainted and elaborately decorated serving pieces.

The Importance of Marks: Factory and Decorator

Marks—a special symbol of a particular factory placed on the back of an object during the manufacturing process—are commonly used to identify porcelain. Collectors and dealers usually look at the mark on a piece of china immediately, even though the eye may have told them what type of porcelain the piece is or who the decorator was. The mark is their reassurance. Most Limoges factories did not routinely mark their products until the latter quarter of the nineteenth century, although several companies did occasionally use marks from the 1850s (d'Albis and Romanet, p. 237).

Marks found on Limoges pieces from the nineteenth century and early twentieth century consist of initials or names of companies written in a certain way and often contained within a special emblem. Sometimes the mark consists of a symbol with no identifying name or initial. Marks indicating that a certain factory made the object are usually stamped under the glaze on the back of the piece. This mark is often in green, or sometimes the mark is incised into the porcelain. Often there is more than one mark on the back of china. Confusion can exist if one does not know what each mark means. In addition to the factory mark, referred to as the white ware mark, there can be marks to indicate factory or studio decoration, importers, exporters, and artists. These other marks are usually over the glaze. By running one's finger over the marks one can determine this. Marks indicating factory decoration are usually in a different color (often red) from the factory white ware mark. American decorating firms or art studios such as Pickard placed their mark with their name on the pieces they decorated. The French (Paris or Limoges) decorating studios were more likely to use marks with symbols or initials and not to use complete names. It can thus be difficult without research to know if the mark is that of a factory or a decorator. There is often more than one factory mark. Many factories decorated white wares manufactured by other companies. Some factories were decorating firms before they began producing porcelain, and the same mark may have been continued. However, in most cases, upon examination of and familiarity with the marking system, one is able to tell for example that one mark stands for the company of manufacture (the one under the glaze), and a second mark stands for decoration (factory, studio, individual). David Haviland, in fact, is credited with implementing the unique "double" marking practice used by most Limoges factories after 1876.

A third mark stands for the exporter (in France) or the importer (in America or other country being either a distributor or commercial business). Pieces which have only a white ware mark tell us one of two things: the piece is early having been decorated in Paris or Limoges before the decoration process became a part of the factory process, or that the piece was sold as a white ware and decorated in this country by a nonprofessional artist. The style and quality of decoration are points in determining this. Artist's signatures are usually found on the front of pieces, sometimes they are hidden and one must look closely to find the mark. Some artists used a special mark on the bottom of the piece. Many times, of course, one sees a name written on the bottom of a piece, with or without a date. This type of signature is common on white wares decorated by nonprofessional artists.

The marks of exporters cannot always be differentiated easily from those of Limoges decorating marks. If there is an overglaze mark, however, it can usually be assumed that the piece was decorated at a Limoges factory or decorating studio. Lack of an overglaze decorating mark does not always indicate that the piece was not decorated at a Limoges factory or decorating studio. Marks could have been omitted by error, and it is not uncommon for all pieces in a set of dinner ware to lack double marks. This is especially true for cups.

The importer marks usually are easily interpreted. They contain the name of a specific department or jewelry store. Sometimes, though, marks for individuals who ordered a specific set of china will be found in conjunction with the factory underglaze and overglaze marks. In the section on marks, I have tried to indicate by company the type of marks used: white ware mark; decorated ware mark; exporter mark; or importer mark.

It is generally accepted that if a mark contains the name of the country of origin the piece was made after 1891. The United States government enacted the McKinley Tariff Law stating that articles imported to this country after 1891 must include the name of the country where they were produced. So theoretically, if the mark contains the word "France," the piece was made after 1891. There are exceptions to this rule, however, for some companies did use "France" in their marks prior to 1891. Also note that while the white ware marks may contain the word "France" the decorating marks usually only include "Limoges," even those decorating marks which are after 1891.

While it is common to see "Made in" as part of English marks, the wording is not routinely found on Limoges marks. I discussed this in the first edition, indicating that such wording implied that the piece was made after 1914 in accordance again with tariff laws. Further examination of Limoges marks, however, clearly indicates that "Made in France," is rarely found on Limoges items made after 1914 until World War II. It is more commonly found on items made after 1945.

Déposé is often found in conjunction with Limoges marks. The French word means "patented." Some Limoges marks, however, actually have "Patent" written or abbreviated in English as part of the mark and include the date when a certain mold or pattern was registered. Bear in mind when seeing such a mark (Pat'd. Nov. 12, 1892, for example), that the date does not indicate that the piece was actually made in 1892. The date only indicates when the design was first copyrighted, and the piece may, in fact, have been made quite a few years later.

In some instances I have found dates of marks attributed to the very first time that a factory was in production at a certain location, even though that factory had changed owners and marks over a long period of time. For example, several sources show that the GDA (see Gérard, Dufraisseix, and Abbot) mark goes back to 1798; in fact the GDA company was established circa 1900. This confusing error results from the fact that the GDA company can be traced back to the old Alluaud firm which actually began in 1798. But it is certainly not accurate to identify a GDA mark on an object as dating from 1798.

Factories did change hands. In fact, this seems to be more the rule than the exception. Sometimes the same marks were continued by the succeeding firms. In most cases the marks changed either completely, or were either altered in some fashion, or a new white ware mark was introduced while the former firm's decorating mark was continued. Also when a certain year is given as the date of a certain mark, that does not mean that all pieces having that mark were made in that one year. The date indicates when the company started using a particular mark. It is often difficult to pinpoint specific dates when a certain mark was used. The approximate time period when a mark was used or when a company was in production is more helpful. Dates for the majority of marks in this book are for approximate time periods. It is also important to realize that a decorating mark may be some years later than the white ware mark on a piece. Items could be manufactured and marked with the factory mark and then placed in stock to be decorated as the need arose. That also can account for finding the same molds with marks of two different companies, usually one mark belongs to the factory which succeeded the other, such as Bernardaud (B&Co.) taking over Délinières (D&Co.).

There are many beautiful examples of hard paste porcelain which have no marks at all. Many of the older Limoges companies and other European hard paste manufacturers did not mark their wares. To collectors this is often exasperating. If the object is not marked Limoges, however, one cannot definitely tell if it is actually Limoges porcelain or porcelain from some other area, like Bavaria, Austria, or Japan. (Of course, some pieces in a set of china might not have the mark on every piece.) For unmarked items, the type of object and style of decoration should give an indication of when it was made, but that is usually all one can say. Unmarked articles do not sell as quickly as marked ones. This is often not a deterrent to a buyer if the piece fits in with one's collection, and if one is not too concerned about its value appreciating.

Often one is cautioned in general not to rely totally on

marks as a method of identification. Many porcelain marks have been copied. The more demand for a particular type of porcelain, the more scarce it becomes on the market. As a result, the possibilities are increased that the marks will be copied on reproductions of those objects. When the first edition was written, there was no problem with fake Limoges marks. A few years later, however, modern pieces made in Taiwan began to appear at flea markets and were offered by wholesale houses specializing in reproductions. Such pieces were marked with a *fleur de lys* and a banner underneath containing the words "Limoges China." The pieces with such a mark are obviously new, and the marks do not resemble the old Limoges marks. There is only one mark, not a separate factory mark and a decorating mark. Undoubtedly, though, such pieces will be sold in the future as "old Limoges" in the same way similar reproductions with misleading marks are sold as Flow Blue china or R.S. Prussia. I suppose one can say that "Limoges" has really "arrived" as a collecting category when efforts are made to fool the collecting public. While I am glad that the number of Limoges collectors has increased, I do regret seeing the arrival of such misleading pieces on the market.

One should also be aware that due to the popularity of Limoges porcelain some English and American earthenware companies used the name "Limoges" in their marks. One should not be confused by this however, for the earthenware items will not meet the prime characteristic of hard paste porcelain; the earthenware *will not* be translucent.

The "repro" problem is basically a very small area of concern for today's Limoges collector. The supply of collectable Limoges and Haviland porcelain products has been adequate. The majority of pieces on the American antiques market today date from the latter part of the 1800's and are just now coming into the classification of "true" antiques, over one hundred years old. Another deterrent for copying Limoges marks is that some of the companies are still in production. The manufacture of porcelain in Limoges is still a large industry. Modern table china and decorative items from Limoges are seen in department stores and gift shops in the United States today. These modern wares, even if produced by companies whose origins date back to the mid 1800s, are not difficult to differentiate from the old. The type of decoration and marks are a help in distinguishing the old from the new. In new table china some of the traditional designs are followed, but in new decorative accessories, often seen in gift shops and flea markets, the colors are usually not as rich, but most importantly, the gold in the trim and embellishments is not applied as lavishly. The gold does not have the rich patina of the earlier pieces.

Marks on the modern pieces are also different. There is usually only one mark with no differentiation between factory manufactured and factory decorated, although the pieces are factory decorated. The practice of decorating the china at the factory has now been going on so long that there is really no need to double mark. The marks have a

"newer" appearance, being more elaborate in form and containing more information than the older, more simple, marks. Many of the gift items are marked only "Limoges, France." Several companies operating during the nineteenth century also marked their products in this way. Often this type of marking today is in gold. Gold marks were quite rare during the earlier period. Also the earlier marking "Limoges, France" appears under the glaze, whereas the newer markings are most often over the glaze. For identifying porcelain objects manufactured during the nineteenth and early twentieth centuries at Limoges, marks are helpful.

In the photograph sections, the marks on the pieces are identified so that by referring to the specific company in the Marks section, one can see the actual mark or marks on the objects illustrated. The majority of marks shown here have an example in the photographs. Some marks, however, have been included which do not have pieces shown in the photograph section. Those marks are given for reference purposes. The majority of the marks were photographed from objects, but some have remained hand drawn because they were not available for photographing. This was done to show a more complete chronology of marks for some of the companies. The marks follow the section listing the Limoges factories and are arranged alphabetically by factory and numbered sequentially for each factory. Please check the Index of Manufacturers if in doubt about the name of the factory.

The Importance of Decoration: Technique and Styles

Decorating techniques changed through the years for the Limoges porcelain industry. Examples of Limoges porcelain found today on the American antiques market, however, appear in one of four categories: (1) unpainted (white ware or blanks), (2) handpainted, (3) transfer decorated, and (4) mixed (a combination of transfer design and handpainted). Decoration may be over or under the glaze. All categories except the first may be further subdivided into factory decorated, studio (professionally) decorated, or individually decorated (amateur or nonprofessional).

Unpainted porcelain does not mean absence of decoration. The article was not "blank" as the term for this type of ware implies. On the contrary, intricate and beautiful designs were molded, incised, or applied to the object in the paste form. Pieces were elaborately fashioned with scalloped borders, scroll work, beading, and fancily shaped handles, knobs, and feet were applied or molded into the piece which in turn might have detailed designs. One can inspect a color decorated object to see or feel the design.

Early Limoges porcelain was not decorated until the entire manufacturing process was completed. The white wares or blanks were sent to Paris and handpainted by artists and studios of that city. This type of decoration was over the glaze. It was fine for decorative objects, but it was not very suitable for articles that would come into contact with much use or handling, specifically table china. Decoration over the glaze although done with vitreous paints and refired to "set" the decoration eventually shows signs of wear if used frequently like with a knife and fork. Pieces subjected to such use can be ruined over a period of time. Objects decorated under the glaze, that is, decoration applied to the bisque form of the piece before the glaze is applied, never show any sign of deterioration—the glaze cannot be penetrated. Objects decorated under the glaze have the vitreous or glassy look all over; they feel smooth to the touch; one cannot feel the painted decoration. Over the glaze, it can be felt; the design has a texture separate from the body of the piece. The appearance is not "slick" as is the case with decoration under glaze. Examine a handpainted vase, for example. If the decoration feels the same as the inside of the vase, the decoration is under the glaze; if it does not, it is over the glaze. Decoration under the glaze was not perfected in the Limoges porcelain industry until the late 1800s.

Décalcomanie is the French term for transfer decoration. A design is made on copper plates or stones in certain colors. The design is pressed onto paper which in turn is pressed onto another object, thus transferring the design to that object. The same design can be used over and over again. Transfer designs are a less expensive process of decoration than handpainting. This method of decoration was popular in England from the late 1700s. English potters were able to use this type of decoration under the glaze successfully before the Limoges hard paste factories. English earthenwares were fired at much lower temperatures in the glaze firing than is required for hard paste porcelain. The potters did not have the problem of the designs melting or running together during this second firing. Transfer decoration can also be applied over the glaze; however, the durability of the design is variable. Once the technique had been perfected of keeping the design intact during the glaze firing, this type of decoration was widely used by the Limoges companies, especially for table china.

Mixtion, the French term implying a mixed technique of decoration, was another popular decorating method. Designs were applied in outline or full (colored) form by the transfer method and then filled in or trimmed by handpainting. This style of decoration could be applied either over or under the glaze. Many decorative accessories and serving china show evidence of this particular technique.

Close examination is often necessary in order to differentiate between the categories of methods of decoration: (1) handpainted; (2) transfer; (3) mixed. Items entirely handpainted are the easiest to determine. Most are painted over the glaze. They have a texture to the touch. Brush strokes and irregularities can be seen when one looks closely. Transfer designs on patterns of table china are usually under the glaze. The pattern is regular and the same on each piece. The design cannot be felt. Pieces decorated by the mixed technique either over or under the glaze are the most difficult to determine. A magnifying glass enables better inspection, when in doubt, than the eye alone. A pattern of raised dots composing the design or a design pattern outline showing no irregularities indicate that the transfer method has been used.

To summarize, white wares, or unpainted Limoges china, are seen on today's market primarily in the form of table china. Although large amounts of the blanks were exported, one rarely sees an undecorated piece in the form of decorative accessories. The white wares were sold to be decorated, and apparently most were decorated by individuals or art studios. Most examples are handpainted. Early Limoges porcelain was decorated by hand in Paris. From the mid 1800s Limoges porcelain was decorated by special decorating firms or at the factory. Handpainting, transfer, and mixed techniques were all employed. From circa 1870 to the late 1920s the transfer and mixed methods were used most frequently for table china. Handpainting during this period was primarily reserved for art objects and decorative pieces.

The style of the early decoration of Limoges porcelain consisted largely of gold designs or themes of flowers and people. The "rose de Limoges" is noted as the chief distinction of the early factories. However decoration tended to reflect the artistic tastes of the historical period. The height of the art nouveau period coincided with the height of the golden age of the Limoges porcelain industry—late 1880s to circa 1905. Although the Art Deco period dates from 1925 because of the Paris exhibition entitled "Arts Decoratif " held that year, examples of that style are seen in pieces of Limoges porcelain dating from the early 1900s.

Floral decor on decorative accessories and art objects, especially roses in all varieties and colors, appears as the most prevalent style of decoration that one sees on Limoges objects. Fruit themes of berries, cherries, and grapes appear as the second most popular form of decoration. Game birds and marine life subjects are evident, especially on elaborate sets of serving china for game, fish and oysters. Figural, both portrait and allegorical, as well as scenic decor are less common than the other themes.

These various styles of decoration are distinguished by deep and vivid colors and embellishments of gold. There are few objects categorized as decorative accessories or art objects that are decorated in delicate or pale tones. Table china is more likely to be decorated in delicate styles, although table china manufactured by Limoges companies other than Haviland often has a bold and colorful design. Gold trim is of course the second chief characteristic of much Limoges porcelain. The gold, referred to as coin gold, was lavishly applied to decorative objects and also to table china during the height of the Limoges porcelain industry. The gold has a rich patina which accents and serves as an outline on the pieces. Objects decorated in such a fashion, especially those professionally handpainted, with vivid floral, fruit, and figural themes, enhanced with gold, are unique and works of art.

Evaluating Limoges Porcelain For Collectors

For the typical American collector of European hard paste porcelain (Limoges, Austrian, Bavarian), there is usually no attempt to stick zealously to the rule that an item must be over 100 years old before it can be considered worthwhile for collection or investment. The first Limoges hard paste production occurred only a little more than 200 years ago, and the Limoges products that have been available through export to the American consumer have been available for only about 150 years. Other European hard paste porcelain also has been produced for less than three hundred years, making the porcelain items "young" by European standards of antiquity. Age is important, of course, but porcelain objects which have survived for 50 to 100 years indicate the quality and desirability of the objects. Porcelain is durable, but it is vulnerable to breakage, much more so than some other categories of antiques and collectables such as furniture. Pieces of porcelain which exist from earlier times show that they have been cared for. The pieces were prized when they were new; they were kept and handed down to future generations. History is preserved: owning a particular piece, whether one inherits or purchases the item, allows one to understand, respect, and share a part of the past. For investment purposes, the objects appreciate in value as years are added to their age.

Marks can be beneficial in determining the approximate age of many pieces of Limoges porcelain. Quality of craftsmanship of the body of the article and quality of decoration on the body of the piece are also important factors to consider in addition to age. The thinness (translucency) of a piece of porcelain sometimes is considered as an indication of quality. Of course, European hard paste porcelains are all translucent; however, they are not "eggshell" thin as some Chinese and Japanese pieces. Examples of Limoges hard paste porcelain represent quality craftsmanship, but there are basically little differences in the thickness among the wares of the different Limoges companies, although some companies' products may be more elaborately or exquisitely fashioned than others. The hard paste products should have a deep bell-like ring when gently tapped. If the piece has a break or "hairline" the sound will be dull. Dealers often exhibit this quality of porcelain items to purchasers in order to show that the piece is perfect when sold.

The type and quality of decoration on pieces of Limoges porcelain vary. The marks, or lack of marks, on pieces of Limoges porcelain often give us a clue to how the pieces were decorated (see section on marks). Handpainted objects with only one mark (white ware mark) under the glaze indicates that a certain factory made the piece, but that the decoration was applied by someone else. That decorator could be either a professional French artist or an amateur or professional American artist. If the piece is signed, the name may give a clue as to the origin of the artist. Handpainted pieces having a mark in addition to the white ware mark, usually over the glaze, indicates that the piece was professionally decorated either by a Limoges (or Paris) studio, a Limoges factory, or by a firm in America (or other country), such as a jewelry company that monogrammed items or by an art school or studio.

Pieces decorated by the mixed technique primarily have the decorating mark of a factory or decoration studio in addition to the white ware mark. Examples are seen which have been both factory decorated and individually decorated—another form of mixed decor. Plates, bowls, platters, and trays frequently are decorated in this manner. The border glaze or pattern may be the finished product of some factory and show a mark for factory decoration, but the middle or inside of the piece, which was unpainted when it left the factory, may be painted with some scene, theme, or monogram at a later time by someone else, professional or nonprofessional. Again if the art work is signed, origin of that particular decoration might be determined.

Pieces decorated by the transfer method are primarily found in examples of table china. Many dinnerware items, however, especially serving pieces, would be considered as a type of mixed decoration, having trim, handles, and feet handpainted with gold. Additionally many transfer designs are often touched up or filled in by hand. Transfer design pieces usually show white ware marks and decorator marks. Sometimes pieces of Limoges porcelain only show a Limoges decorator's mark signifying that the company that manufactured the item did not use a white ware mark. We do not consider the piece unmarked however as the decorating mark indicates Limoges. Other pieces having no white ware mark but a decorating mark that cannot be attributed to Limoges, like Pickard, for example, are not considered Limoges even though the decoration may represent the Limoges image.

Limoges art objects and decorative accessories primarily are handpainted or of mixed decor, as described in the earlier section on decorating techniques. The amount of individual work that goes into the decoration of an object usually serves as the criterion of superiority.

When prices were revised in 1984, I set up a key identifying the type of decoration for each piece. The prices were coded to indicate whether the piece had professional French decoration either by factory or decorating studio (FD); professional American decoration by a specific American decorating studio (PD); quality decoration by a professional or non-professional artist for pieces which did not have either a French or an American decorating mark (QD); amateur decoration by an American non-professional china painter (AD); and undecorated white ware, or blanks (UD). Differentiating between the several methods of decoration found on Limoges porcelain is necessary, especially for the serious and advanced collector. There is a very wide variation in quality for items decorated in America. The prices in the first edition reflected a range within which Limoges porcelain could be obtained at that time, often a large dollar range for pieces of similar quality. Also, some French decorated pieces were priced considerably lower than some pieces decorated by amateur American painters. Such unequal pricing is not nearly so common today. Astute dealers and collectors are now aware of the different values and use this knowledge in pricing their Limoges. Today, Limoges prices fit the pieces much more closely to quality and origin of decoration than was the case ten years ago.

I elaborated on this system of evaluating Limoges by quality of decoration in an article written for *The Antique Trader Weekly* (July 3, 1985, pp. 56-60). Basically Limoges can be rated on the basis of origin and type of decoration, which can be determined by its marks. First, the most desirable pieces are those which have been handpainted in Limoges factories or decorating studios in Limoges or Paris. Examples will have at least two marks, one underglaze and one overglaze. Some pieces may have an artist's signature or initials on the front of the piece. Sometimes, an artist's mark or initial will be on the base or the back of the item. The *Mixtion* type of decoration, for example transfers of portraits or cherubs with partial handpainted work, is also included in this first category. But these examples are valued less than the totally handpainted pieces. Many of the more collectible pieces with figural, scenic, and portrait decoration, however, are of this type.

Second in desirability are pieces handpainted by American decorating studios. Examples will have two marks, the underglaze Limoges factory mark and the overglaze American studio mark such as Pickard or Stouffer. Such pieces usually have a studio artist's signature on the face.

The third category of collectible Limoges is comprised of pieces with Limoges factory transfer designs or patterns. Examples will have at least two marks, the underglaze factory mark and the overglaze decorating mark of the factory or studio.

The fourth category of Limoges consists of items handpainted by American artists or china painters. Examples will have only one mark, underglaze, denoting the Limoges manufacturing company. Pieces may be signed on the front or on the base. This fourth category is the one which poses the most concern for the discriminating collector. Some of the American handpainted work is clearly of a professional quality and should be considered on the same level, or just below that of American decorating studios. Many other pieces, however, exhibit obviously amateur workmanship, and these should not be priced in the same range just because they are "handpainted."

For this book, I have divided the photographs according to decoration rather than grouping all of the same objects together and thereby mixing the French decorated pieces with the American decorated items. The first category of photographs illustrates French decoration either by factory or studio. The French section is subdivided into several sections according to decoration with brief remarks prefacing the individual groups of pictures.

The second category of photographs is devoted to American decorated Limoges. This category is further divided into three sections according to (1) Professional American Decoration; (2) Quality American Decoration; and (3) Amateur American Decoration. Please note that the pieces shown in the latter section may be attractive, but only examples with unquestionably well executed handpainted work were placed under Quality American Decoration.

A few other points to consider when evaluating Limoges should be noted. Some factories were in production for only a short time, thus examples of their wares, however decorated or even unpainted, may be desirable due to scarcity. Some companies did not export to the United States in quantities as large as others, thus their products are scarce. Certain types of objects appear on the market more than others. Decorative plaques, vases, cachepots, tankards, and fish services are well represented. Whiskey decanters, cuspidors, inkwells, humidors, perfume bottles, baskets, jardinieres, pancake dishes—to name just a few—are not so prevalent. The serving or extra pieces to dinner services such as tea and coffee pots, butter pats, butter dishes, and bone dishes as well as cups for place settings make these items desirable if needed to complete a set even though the majority are transfer decorated. Certain themes of decoration such as scenic and animal are more scarce than the other themes. Pieces signed by a specific artist, either professional or in some cases nonprofessional, are often in demand. Determining the specific desirability of Limoges porcelain for individual collection and investment comes through study and experience: reading, looking, touching, examining, and deciding what is personally appealing.

The variety of Limoges porcelain available today provides many ideas for collections. Collections can range from the very general to the very specific. A wide selection of decorative pieces manufactured by different Limoges companies, decorated in different styles by different techniques allows one to enjoy and sample a beautiful array of Limoges porcelain. Personal creativity in putting together a collection for pleasure, investment, or both can be an enjoyable and worthwhile endeavor.

Photographs

French Decoration–Art Objects

In the broad category of French factory or studio decorated Limoges, the first group of photographs features Art Objects. These are items made solely for exhibiting, and they are usually highly decorated. Examples are often large items such as vases, urns, and jardinieres. Paintings on porcelain, either framed or mounted, are also in this category. It is really quite rare to find these kinds of pieces with French decoration. Most examples are blanks handpainted by American artists. While the American decoration may sometimes appear quite professional, without an artist's signature, or a factory or studio decorator mark, it is impossible to definitely attribute the origin of decoration to Limoges. (See examples of this in the first section of photographs under American Decoration.)

Several Gúerin, Pouyat, and Haviland factory decorated vases are shown in this first section as well as a few pieces of Haviland art pottery. The latter are not "Limoges Porcelain," technically, but they have been included because of their unique nature.

Limoges urns are quite rare, and a very lovely one exported by Straus is featured. Decorative plates and cherub decor are usually considered as "Decorative Objects," but a superb set of three plates decorated by Ahrenfeldt have been defined as art objects here. Handpainted figural and portrait chargers or plaques are differentiated from similarly decorated or smaller plates or plaques. The latter are placed under Decorative Objects unless the decoration or nature of design causes the piece to merit the higher classification of Art Object. The Levy (Imperial) plate with a mythological scene is one example of a plate warranting art object status.

Tankards are seldom found with factory decoration, and they are generally categorized as decorative table wares. One by Pouyat, decorated with a nude figure, is obviously an Art Object, however. An unusual T&V decorated pitcher portraying semi-nudes also has been placed in this first section.

Two ormolu mounted pieces, a portrait bowl by Merlin-Lemas and a floral decorated server by an unidentified Limoges factory, are other examples of Art Objects. The section concludes with two pieces of White House china made by Haviland and Company and decorated after the designs of Theo. R. Davis. While originally designed for use, the rarity of such pieces automatically puts them under the Art Object classification.

PLATE 1: Vase, 15"h, handpainted irises on green background, gold trim. Gúerin Marks 3 and 4 in green.

PLATE 2

PLATE 3

PLATE 2: Portrait Charger, 18"d, handpainted Dutch girls with scenic sea side background, artist signed "DuBois," irregular border heavily gilded. Flambeau China (LDB&C) Mark 2 in red.

PLATE 3: Portrait Charger, 17½"d, handpainted figural and scenic decoration with a biblical theme: woman giving money to child with onlookers in background, scrolled border with embossed work painted gold, artist signed "DuBois." Flambeau China (LDB&C) Mark 2 in blue.

PLATE 4: Palace Urn, 29"h, handpainted figural courtship decor, courtly dress: man kneeling and playing a flute while seated woman is about to place a garland of flowers on his head, artist signed "Gayou." Straus (LS&S) Mark in red.

PLATE 5

PLATE 6

PLATE 7

PLATES 5, 6, and 7: Decorative Plates, set of three, 9½"d, very fancy borders with deeply embossed scroll work extending into plates (note difference in gold application on each border), cherubs in clouds decorate center of each plate. V.F. Mark in green and C.J. Ahrenfeldt Mark 1 in blue.

23

PLATE 8: Vase, 13"h, gold paste roses and leaves on dark cobalt blue finish, high glaze, Guérin Marks 3 in green and 4 in blue.

PLATE 9

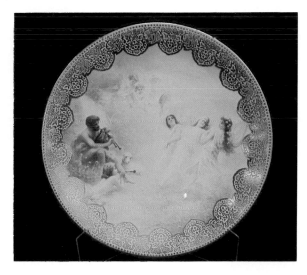

PLATE 10

PLATE 9: Decorative Portrait Plaque, 12"d, woman with golden brown hair dressed in flowing pink gown, artist signed " Triple." Lazeyras, Rosenfeld, & Lehman Mark 3 in green.

PLATE 10: Decorative Plate, 9½"d, handpainted mythological figural scene: women dancing while men play musical instruments, children in clouds in background, wide gold border with etched designs frames painting, artist signed "A. Sanstre." Limoges, France Mark 6 in green and Levy (Imperial) Mark in red.

PLATE 11

PLATE 13

PLATE 12

PLATE 11: Vase, 12½"h, applied twisted shaped handles, large pink and white roses on white body. Latrille Frères Mark in green and Bawo & Dotter Mark 8 in red.

PLATE 12: Vase, 12"h, large gold paste flowers, stems, and leaves highlighted with turquoise enamelled beading in the form of small flowers and studding the center of the larger gold blossoms, artist signed "H. Joie." Limoges, France Mark 6 in green and P. Pastaud Mark in gold.

PLATE 13: Vase, 14"h, handpainted figural decor of two semi-nude women, artist signed, "E. Furlaud." Pouyat Mark 5 in green and Mark 9 in pink and green with "Peint et Doré à la main a Limoges" in green.

PLATE 14

PLATE 15

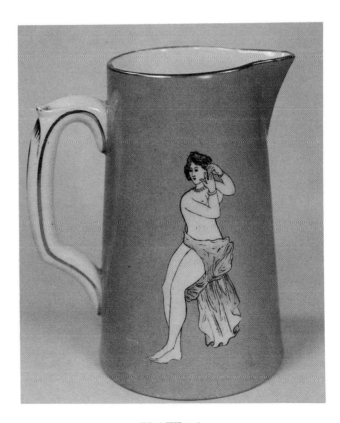

PLATE 16

PLATE 14: Portrait Tankard, 13"h, handpainted nude woman holding water jug over left shoulder. Pouyat Marks 5 in green and Mark 9 in pink and green.

PLATE 15: Portrait Pitcher, 6½"h, handpainted figural semi-nudes, on deep pink background, in an Art Deco style with Egyptian influence decorate both sides of pitcher; the first view portrays a woman draped in blue gazing at a compact (see second view in following photograph). This piece is marked "France," underglaze in green, with T&V Mark 11 in red.

PLATE 16: Reverse side of Porterait Pitcher; seated figure in yellow drape, seemingly putting on an earring (note other jewelry).

PLATE 17

PLATE 18

PLATE 17: Portrait Plate, 9½"d, mounted in gilded metal footed compote, artist signed "G. Kow." Merlin-Lemas Marks 1 in green and 2 in red.

PLATE 18: Server, 12"l, mounted on footed gilded metal base with applied bird and branch; handpainted red flowers with blue ribbon decorate center, shaded pink background on heavily embossed body; artist signed "EP." Limoges, France Mark 2 in green, no decorating mark, but piece exhibits professional French decoration.

28

PLATE 19

PLATE 20

PLATES 19 and 20: Jardiniere, 5½"h, 9½"d, deeply scalloped four-footed base, swan neck handles, figural cupids decorate one side while children fishing are shown on the opposite side, pale blue background, heavy gold trim. Bawo & Dotter Mark 8 in red, no white ware mark.

PLATE 21: Morning Glory Vase, 6"h, an example of early Haviland decoration, circa mid 1850s. H&CO. Mark 4.

PLATE 22

PLATE 24

PLATE 23

PLATE 25

PLATE 22: Stoneware Tankard, 12"h, black and gold star designs on brown-toned body, artist signed "A.D." H&CO. Mark 22.

PLATE 23: Double Vase, 13¼"w, 9"h, divided opening, art pottery with a high glaze, bird and floral decor on blue-green background. H&CO. Mark 20.

PLATE 24: Vase, 11½"h, art pottery with silver alloy base, high glaze, flower and leaves decor. H&CO. Mark 21 (impressed inside top lip of vase).

PLATE 25: Vase, 10⅝"h, art pottery, pink and white roses on shaded blue-green background. H&CO. Mark 20.

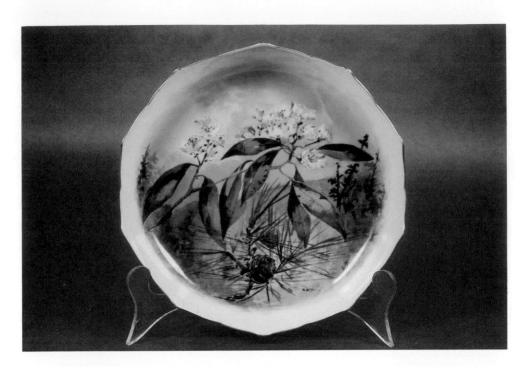

PLATE 26

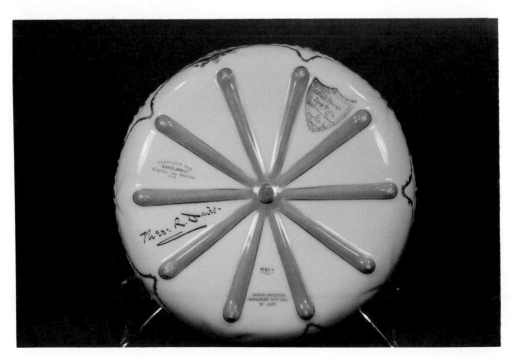

PLATE 27

PLATE 26: Presidential China, Soup Plate, 9"d, an example from the Hays' service made by Haviland. The decoration was made from designs by Theo R. Davis patented in 1880.

PLATE 27: Bottom of Soup Plate in preceding photograph showing the different marks on the piece. Note also the raised enamelled spokes.

PLATE 28

PLATE 29

PLATE 28 Leaf Bowl, 12"d, another example made by Haviland from a design by Theo. R. Davis patented in 1880. This piece exhibits a garden theme with red fruit, beetle, and a rabbit.

PLATE 29: Base of Leaf Bowl in preceding photograph showing the various marks on the piece, including the signature of Davis and the U.S. Eagle and Laurel Branch insignia.

French Decoration–Decorative Objects

The second section of French factory or studio decorated Limoges is large, chiefly composed of decorative items, most intended more for display purposes than for use. The pieces shown in this section do not include repetitive transfer patterns commonly found on table wares and some dresser items.

This section is divided into three parts based on outstanding and colorful decoration. Portrait and Figural themes are presented first, followed by Fruit and Flowers. Some Abstract Designs precede Scenic Views. Fish and Game subjects complete the first part of this section. The decoration on the majority of these pieces is characterized by vivid colors, heavy gold trim, and an artist's signature (either by the person who painted the piece or who executed the design). The decoration is either handpainted or *Mixtion*. Many of the portrait pieces as well as others are, in fact, an example of this latter method, combining handpainting with transfer outlines. The Borgfeldt (Coronet) Cavalier plates are just one example. The majority of items in this first part are plates, plaques, or small vases, but table ware items such as baskets, cups, biscuit jars, and so forth are also included here because of decoration.

The second part of this section focuses on more delicately decorated pieces. Again, these are examples of studio or factory decoration which are not repetitive table ware patterns. Many of these items are table wares, but the decoration is unique to the piece. There may be a set of cups or oyster plates with the same decoration, but the number of such sets would be limited, and hand work by a French decorator was employed. Cherubs, Figural and Floral Cameos, and Floral Designs are illustrated in this part.

Two other types of decoration compose the third and last part of this section: Monochrome and Gold. Monochrome colors with gold or only gold decoration is simple, but often quite attractive. Moreover, these types of decoration are hand applied and merit inclusion here based on origin and type of decoration. Early Limoges decoration was simple with only gold trim or colored bands as shown by several early serving pieces. Monochromes such as cobalt blue and wine or rose, accentuated by gold, are also quite striking and very collectible.

Portrait and Figural Themes

PLATE 30. Figural Plaque, 10"d, courtship scene of couple in garden, courtly dress, artist signed, "Lancy." SW Mark in red.

PLATE 31

PLATE 32

PLATE 31: Figural Charger, 15½"d, courtship scene of couple in garden, Napoleonic dress, artist signed, "Mirelle." LR&L Mark 2 in red.

PLATE 32: Figural Plate, 10½"d, courtship scene of couple seated in garden, vivid colors, artist signed, "Valentine." LR&L Mark 2 in green.

PLATE 33: Figural Charger, 14"d, court scene with gentleman preparing to be barbered or shaved, artist signed, "DuBois." Limoges, France Mark 8 in blue.

PLATE 33

PLATE 34

PLATE 35

PLATE 34: Figural Charger, 15½"d, street scene with figures in eighteenth century dress, heavily gilded rococo border, artist signed (illegible). LR&L Mark 2 in red.

PLATE 35: Portrait Plate, 10"d, garden scene with woman dressed in long white gown with an apricot sash; wide cobalt blue border overlaid with elaborate gold work, artist signed, "J. Soustre." H&CO. Mark 11 with "Floreal Gold" and "Haviland and Co. pour E. Offner, New Orleans."

PLATE 36

PLATE 37

PLATE 36: Portrait Plate, 9½"d, mythological figure holding crescent moon against stars in the background; wine border decorated with gold stencilled designs. H&CO. Mark 12 in green, no decorating mark, but the transfer figure and border decoration indicates professional French decoration, but probably not by the Haviland Company.

FIGURE 37: Plate, 8"d, figural portrait of a woman in Victorian dress surrounded by a winter scene. The plate is heavily scalloped with a fluted inner border, all richly decorated in gold. Latrille Mark 1 in green and Straus Mark in blue.

PLATE 38

PLATE 40

PLATE 39

PLATE 41

PLATE 38: Portrait Plate, 10"d, woman standing in courtyard holding a flower, biblical style dress. LR&L Mark 2 in red.

PLATE 39: Figural Plaque, 10½"d, harbor scene with woman standing and child sitting on wall with her arms around the woman's neck. Limoges, France Mark 4 in green, no decorating mark.

PLATE 40: Portrait Plaque, 10½"d, woman with long brown hair dressed in an off-shoulder orange drape against a dark to light burnt-orange background, signed "Puisoyes." LR&L Mark 3 in gray.

PLATE 41: Cavalier Plate, 10½"d, pierced to hang, vividly painted portrait of a smiling cavalier, artist signed "L. Coudert" Mavaleix Mark in green and Borgfeldt Mark 1 in green.

PLATE 42

PLATE 43

PLATE 42: Cavalier Plate, 10"d, standing figure dressed in a yellow tunic with a purple cape, artist signed "Luc." Borgfeldt Mark 2 in blue.

PLATE 43: Cavalier Plate, 10"d, seated figure dressed in colorful costume, border enhanced with gold, artist signed, "La Pie." Borgfeldt Mark 1 in green.

PLATE 44: Cavalier Plate, 10"d, standing figure dressed in a pink tunic, white shirt, and green cape, artist signed, "Luc." Borgfeldt Mark 1 in blue.

PLATE 44

PLATE 45: Indian Portrait Plate, 9¾"d, figure with long black hair, adorned with hat, beads, and medals, artist signed, "Luc." Borgfeldt Mark 1 in green.

PLATE 46: Portrait Plate, 9½"d, seated woman with basket, dressed in blue jumper and yellow underskirt and hat, artist signed, "Luc." Borgfeldt Mark 1 in blue.

Fruit and Floral

PLATE 47

PLATE 48

PLATE 47: Fruit Plate, 10¾"d, large yellow apples with large pink flowers and green leaves. Flambeau China Marks 1 and 4 in green.

PLATE 48: Floral Plate, 11½"d, multi-colored dahlias in large basket, artist signed, "DuVal," Borgfeldt Mark 1 in blue.

PLATE 49: Fruit Plate, 10¼"d, sliced orange and purple grapes on shaded green background, artist signed, "Barbet." Borgfeldt Mark 1 in green.

PLATE 49

PLATE 50

PLATE 51

PLATE 52

PLATE 50: Ferner, 5½"h, 7"d, footed, pink roses on pale yellow to deep burnt-orange background, heavily gilded feet, artist signed, "Gex." Borgfeldt Mark 1 in green.

PLATE 51: Vase, 8¼"h, applied handles and feet decorated in gold; purple and yellow irises on matte cream background. Redon Mark 2 in green and Bawo & Dotter Mark 8 in red, artist initialed "JRG" in gold on bottom.

PLATE 52: Vase, 8"h, applied flowers and branches form handles which are decorated in green and enhanced with gold; large pink flowers and green buds outlined in gold decorate ivory matte finished body. Redon Mark 1 in green, no decorating mark, but art is of professional French origin.

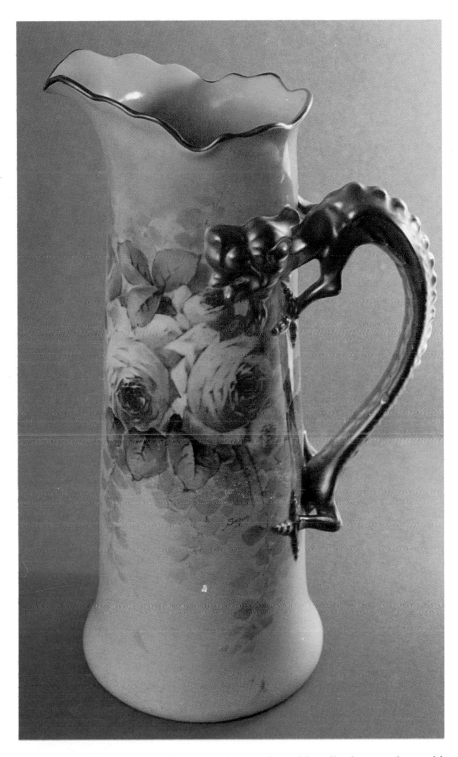

PLATE 53: Floral Tankard, 14½"h, dragon shaped handle decorated in gold; large pink roses with green leaves on pale green background. Pouyat Marks 5 in green and 9 in pink and green.

PLATE 54: Floral Plaque, 11½"d, white and violet tinted flowers on shaded purple background. Limoges, France Mark 2 in green and B&H Mark in green.

PLATE 55: Pancake Dish, underplate, 9½"d, large pink and white roses on shaded blue background, artist signed, "Habemert." Lanternier Mark 4 in green and Limoges Art Porcelaine Co. Mark in blue.

PLATE 56

PLATE 58

PLATE 57

PLATE 59

PLATE 56: Cider Pitcher, 8"d, elaborate two part handle heavily gilded; large red and pink roses on light green background. T&V Marks 7 in green and 16 in purple.

PLATE 57: Chocolate Pot, 10"h, pink floral spray with green leaves on orange body with wide gold band around center. T&V Mark 2 in gold.

PLATE 58: Cider Pitcher, 6"h, pink and white flowers with enamelling on deep turquoise background shading to white; scalloped designs on body and neck and handle painted gold. T&V Mark 5a in green and 15 in purple.

PLATE 59: Cider Pitcher, 6"h, large pink and red roses on shaded blue background, artist signed, "Merenlet." T&V Marks 4a in green and 16 in purple.

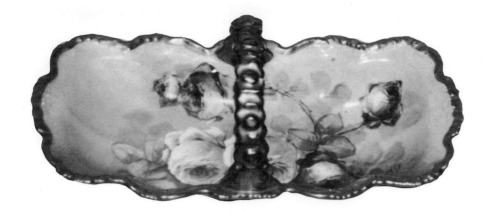

PLATE 60: Basket, 9"x 5", large pink and red roses on shaded cream background, gilded border and handle, artist signed, "DuVal." Pouyat Mark 5 in green, no decorating mark, but art work is by a Limoges artist.

PLATE 61: Dresser Tray, 13"x8½", scrolled rim forms handles, multi-colored roses on lower corner with small white flowers in opposite corner, artist signed, "Vogt." T&V Marks 8 in green and 16 in purple.

PLATE 62: Fruit Bowl, 9¼"d, braided handles, wide blue-green glaze on outer border, center decoration of pears, gold trim. H&CO. Mark 9 in green, no decorating mark, but decoration is of French origin.

PLATE 63

PLATE 64

PLATE 65

PLATE 66

PLATE 67

PLATE 68

PLATE 63: Berry Set: Serving Bowl, 10"d; 6 individual Bowls, 5½"d; pink and wine roses decorate lower portion of bowls, gold trim, artist signed, "André," Coiffe Mark 3 in green and Flambeau China Mark 4 in green.

PLATE 64: Cake Plate, 12"d, large white flowers on shaded green background, gold trim, artist signed, "DuVal." Pouyat Mark 5 in green, no decorating mark, but art is by a Limoges painter.

PLATE 65: Floral Plate, 10½"d, gold flowers and leaves form a six point star outlining center of plate decorated with scattered multi-colored flowers; wide cobalt blue border, beaded gold rim, artist signed, "Ernest Barbeau." H&CO. Mark 12 in green and in gold.

PLATE 66: Floral Plate, 9½"d, large pink roses with white enamelling, gold trim, artist signed, "M. Naudin." H&CO. Marks 12 in green and 13 in red.

PLATE 67: Floral Charger, 12"d, heavily scalloped and beaded border trimmed in gold; small pink roses decorate center and inner border, shaded green background. Coiffe Mark 2 in green and Straus Mark in gray.

PLATE 68: Floral Charger, 12"d, rococo border finished in gold, wide green inner border decorated with pink rose clusters; the inner border outlines a star design with a gold medallion in the center; enamelled gold flowers overlay the star shape. Coiffe Mark 2 in green and Straus Mark in red.

PLATE 69

PLATE 70

PLATE 71

PLATE 72

PLATE 69: Floral Plate, 9½"d, large multi-colored flowers with green leaves on light yellow background decorate center surrounded by deep border with cobalt blue finish, gold trim, artist signed, "Henry." Pouyat Mark 5 in green, no decorating mark but decoration is French.

PLATE 70: Floral Plate, 11"d, large yellow and pink roses, gold scalloped border, artist signed, "Moly," Mavaleix Mark in green and Limoges, France Mark 9 in black.

PLATE 71: Fruit Plate, 8¾"d, white grapes, green and white leaves, gold trim, artist signed, "DuVal." Latrille Marks 1 and 3 in green.

PLATE 72: Floral Bowl, 5"d, yellow and dark pink roses on tinted yellow and green background, artist signed, "Rogin." Legrand Mark in green and LR&L Mark in gray.

PLATE 73

PLATE 74

PLATE 75

PLATE 76

PLATE 73: Floral Plate, 7½"d, delicately fluted border, large pink roses with enamelled work, delicate gold trim. Sazerat Mark 1 in green, no decorating mark, but decoration is French.

PLATE 74: Fruit Plate, 8½"d, strawberries and leaves decorate inner border, gold beaded work on scalloped outer border. Coiffe Mark 3 in green and Flambeau China Mark 4 in green.

PLATE 75: Floral Plate, 8¾"d, red poinsettias with green leaves, gold trim, artist signed, "Lamour." Latrille Marks 1 and 3 in green.

PLATE 76: Fruit Plate, 10"d, peaches and pink blossoms with green leaves form inner border, gold trim. Coiffe Mark 3 in green and Flambeau China Mark 4 in green.

PLATE 77

PLATE 78

PLATE 79

PLATE 80

PLATE 77: Cup, red berries with green leaves decorate both the inside and outside of cup, gold trim, artist signed, "Mary." Lanternier Mark 1 in red, no white ware mark.

PLATE 78: Cup, orange flowers and green leaves, artist signed, "Henri." Lanternier Mark 1 in red, no white ware mark.

PLATE 79: Cup and Saucer, red berries with gold and green leaves on light green background, gold trim, artist signed, "DuVal." Lanternier Mark in red, no white ware mark.

PLATE 80: Covered Sugar Bowl and Creamer, pink flowers and green leaves painted in an Art Nouveau style, gold trim. Latrille Mark 3 in green, no white ware mark.

Abstract Designs and Scenic Views

PLATE 81: Mug, 5½"h, handpainted medallions with black centers alternate with smaller gold medallions connected with a gold chain; black outer border, gold handle, artist signed, "Max." Paroutaud Mark 1 in green and Flambeau China Mark 4 in green.

PLATE 82: Covered Box, 5½"d, orange, yellow, and black circular designs are featured on a green background divided by abstract white lines in an Art Deco style. Serpaut Mark in green and B.S. Mark in green.

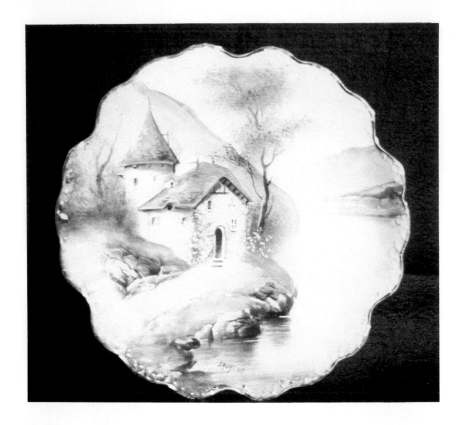

PLATE 83: Scenic Plaque, 10½"d, mill cottage on river bank with mountains in background, artist signed, "Laurent." Bawo & Dotter Marks 5 in green and 9 in red.

PLATE 84: Scenic Plaque, 10½"d, mill cottage on river bank, similar to scene in preceding photograph, but with a view of a bridge, artist signed, "Laurent." Bawo & Dotter Marks 5 in green and 9 in red.

PLATE 85: Scenic Plate, 9"d, windmill on river bank, similar to preceding plaques, artist signed, "E. Vidal." Bawo & Dotter Marks 5 in green and 9 in red.

PLATE 86: Scenic Plate, 10"d, mill on river with trees and mountains in background; yellow flowers and Art Nouveau designs decorate outer border, artist signed, "Lyra." Bawo & Dotter Marks 5 in green and 9 in red with "Handpainted" in gold.

PLATE 87

PLATE 89

PLATE 88

PLATE 87: Scenic Plate, 10"d, black masted boats on blue-gray water; dark sky with a hint of sun peeking through stormy clouds. B&H Mark in green, no white ware mark.

PLATE 88: Scenic Plate, 10"d, two figures in large boat with sail, artist signed, "DuVal." Borgfeldt Mark 1 in green.

PLATE 89: Scenic Plate, 9½"d, pierced and scalloped border; seascape decor in cobalt blue shading to white, gold trim, artist signed, "P. Wallestirz." H&CO. Marks 9 in green and 14 in blue.

PLATE 90

PLATE 91

PLATE 90: Scenic and Floral Plate, 10"d, large orange flowers in foreground with a faint scenic design appearing in the background; deeply scalloped border painted gold. Plainemaison Mark in green and B&H Mark in green.

PLATE 91: Scenic Charger, 13¾"d, Oriental scene decorates center, framed by a large white flower and leaf design outlined in gold on high glazed turquoise background; gold stencilled designs around inner border, gold trim. H&CO. Marks 9 in green and 18 in blue.

PLATE 92: Ice Cream Set: Tray, 13¾"l with 4 Serving Dishes, 5"sq; a winter scene in cameo form is shown on each piece, enhanced by gold floral and leaf designs and enamelled work. GDM Marks 1 in green and 3 in blue.

PLATE 92

Fish and Game

PLATE 93

PLATE 94

PLATE 95

PLATE 96

PLATE 93: Fish Plate, 10"d, a pair of fish on pale blue background are surrounded by large pink blossoms, artist signed, "DuBois." Flambeau China Mark 3 in green, no white ware mark.

PLATE 94: Fish Plate, 9¼"d, single fish with seaweed in foreground; scalloped border with embossed work, artist signed, "Henry." Limoges, France Mark 6 in green and Maas Mark in blue.

PLATE 95: Fish Plate, 10½"d, large fish with purple iris in foreground, artist signed, "Levy." Flambeau China Marks 1 and 3 in green.

PLATE 96: Fish Charger, 12"d, two large fish dominate the scenic lake decor, gold trim, artist signed, "Brisson." Flambeau China Mark 2 in red.

PLATE 97

PLATE 98

PLATE 99

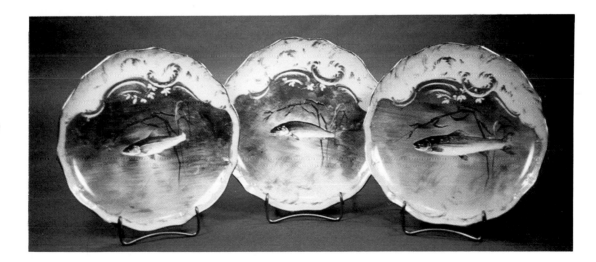

PLATE 97: Fish Platter, 24"l, 9"w, part of a set (individual plates and sauce boat not shown), large fish decorates center of platter with a different fish on each individual plate, blue and green floral border, gold trim. Délinières Marks 2 in green and 4 in red.

PLATE 98: Fish Platter, 22½"l, 10"w, scalloped and beaded edge painted gold, large fish on green background surrounded by water vegetation and shells, artist signed, "Melo." Limoges, France Mark 2 in green and Straus Mark in red.

PLATE 99: Fish Set: Serving Plates, 8½"d, underwater scene with fish in center of each plate; irregular light green border with gold accents. Pouyat Marks 5 in green with a patent date of "Dec. 6, 1898," and Mark 8 in green.

PLATE 100

PLATE 101

PLATE 102

PLATE 100: Fish Platter, 22½"l, matching serving plates in preceding photograph.

PLATE 101: Fish Set: Serving Plates (10), 9½"d, (Sauce Boat and Underplate not shown); small fish with underwater vegetation on pale pink background; fancy

scalloped and floral designs enamelled in gold accentuate the design. Granger Mark 2 in green and LR&L Marks 4 and 5 in blue.

PLATE 102: Fish Platter, 18"l, matching plates in preceding photograph.

58

PLATE 103: Fish Set: Platter, 23"l, Serving Plates (10), 9"d, Gravy Boat with Underplate; scalloped border with shell designs, gold paste flowers, deep pink border, gold trim. CH Mark in green and Bawo & Dotter Mark 6 in red.

PLATE 104: Individual Oyster Dishes (for 1 oyster), 3"d, set of 8, seaweed decor, Délinières Mark 3 in green and Bawo & Dotter Mark 8 in red.

PLATE 105: Fish Set: Platter, 22"l, 12 Serving Plates, 9"d, scalloped shell border, natural colored fish and marine plants decorate outer borders. Lanternier Marks 4 in green and 6 in brown.

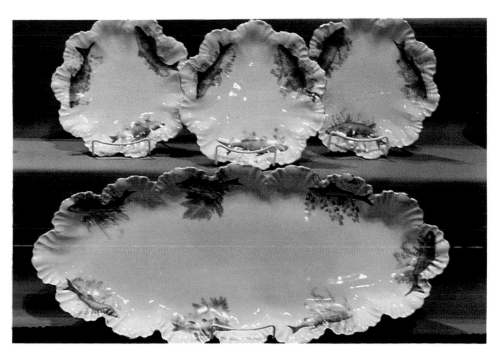

59

PLATE 106: Fish Plate, 9"d, scalloped border, interior shell designs on body decorated with a small fish and underwater plants, gold trim. Redon Marks 2 in green and 3 in red.

PLATE 107: Fish Plates, 9"d, scenic river decor with a large fish in foreground, realistic water and sky coloring. T&V Mark 10 in gold, no white ware mark.

PLATE 108: Fish Plate, 8½"d, fish design in "*Japonnaise*" style, wide blue outer border. H&CO. Marks 9 in green and 18 in blue.

PLATE 109: Game Bird Platter, 18"l, 12"w, from a service for 12 with different birds painted on each plate (serving plates not shown). The platter portrays birds in flight with a scenic view of hunters in a boat; ornately scalloped and gilded inner border with wine outer border, artist signed "DuBois." LR&L Mark 1 in red, no white ware mark.

PLATE 110: Game Bird Set: Platter, 18"l with 12 serving plates, 9¼"d; platter decorated with two ducks in pond, and each serving plate (see plates 110a-110f) painted with a different game bird, framed with gold scrolled designs, brushed gold trim, artist signed, "Genamaud." T&V Marks 8 in green and 16 in purple.

PLATE 110a

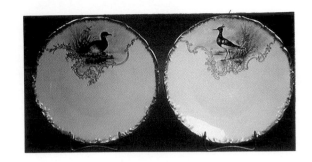

PLATE 110b

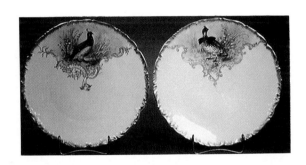

PLATE 110c

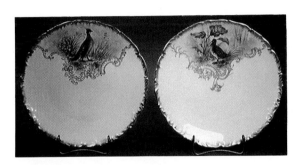

PLATE 110d

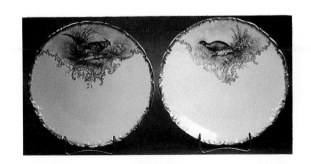

PLATE 110e

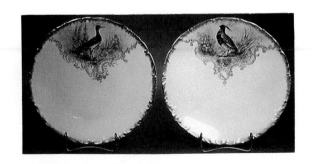

PLATE 110f

PLATE 111

PLATE 113

PLATE 112

PLATE 114

PLATE 111: Game Bird Plaque, 12"d, scalloped and beaded rim trimmed in gold, artist signed, "Henriot." Legrand Mark in green and LR&L Mark 3 in gray with "Handpainted" stamped as part of the mark.

PLATE 112: Pair of Game Bird Plaques, 9½"d, a different bird is shown on each plate with similar background coloring, artist signed, "Max." The plate on the left has Borgfeldt Mark 1 in green; the one on the right has C et J Mark in red, no white ware marks.

PLATE 113: Game Bird Plate, 10½"d, game bird on mixed green and brown background, artist signed (illegible), Limoges, France Mark 3 in green and B&H Mark in green.

PLATE 114: Game Bird Plate, 10"d, scenic decor with bird nestled in the brush, gold trim. Flambeau China Mark 2 in red, no white ware mark.

PLATE 115: Game Bird Plate, 9½"d, rococo border painted gold, brown feathered bird in flight on shaded yellow background, pink flowers in foreground, artist signed (illegible). Flambeau China Mark 4 in green, no white ware mark.

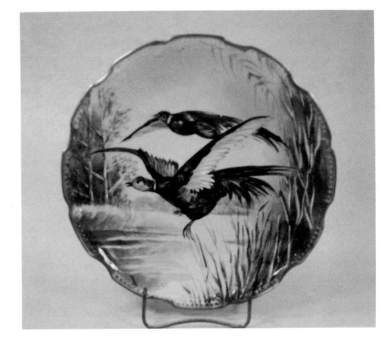

PLATE 116: Game Bird Plate, 9½"d, ring-neck pheasants dominate an outdoor water scene, gold trim, artist signed, "J. Morsey." Latrille Mark 1 in green and Straus Mark in red.

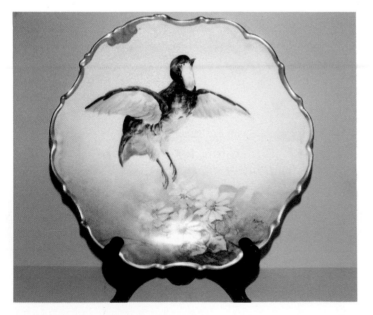

PLATE 117: Game Bird Plate, 10"d, bird poised in flight, white flowers in foreground, gold trim on scalloped border. Flambeau China Marks 1 and 4 in green.

PLATE 118

PLATE 119

PLATE 120

PLATE 121

PLATE 118: Game Bird Plaque, 13½"d, duck flying over lake, artist signed, "Sena." Limoges, France Mark 3 in green and B&H Mark in green.

PLATE 119: Game Bird Plaque, 13½"d, ducks on river bank with scenic view in background; deeply scalloped border trimmed in gold. Redon Marks 2 in green and 4 in red.

PLATE 120: Game Bird Charger, 18"d, one of a pair of chargers, ducks swimming in lake, artist signed, "Max." Pouyat Mark 5 in green, no decorating mark, but artist was a Limoges painter.

PLATE 121: Game Bird Charger, 18"d, matches charger in preceding photograph, pair of ducks in flight over lake.

PLATE 122

PLATE 124

PLATE 123

PLATE 122: Game Bird Plate, 9½"d, black feathered white breasted bird in flight, orange flowers at top of plate, artist signed, "Max." Limoges, France Mark 6 in green and Flambeau China Mark 2 in red.

PLATE 123: Game Bird Plaque, 13"d, pair of game birds, large white flowers in foreground, gold rococo border, artist signed, "Jean." Flambeau China Mark 4 in green, no white ware mark.

PLATE 124: Game Bird Plaque, 13"d, two water fowl in a marsh setting, gold trim, Straus Mark in red, no white ware mark.

PLATE 125: Wild Boar Plate, 10"d, boars cavorting in a winter setting, artist signed "Pradet." Coiffe Mark 2 in green and Borgfeldt Mark 1 in green.

PLATE 126: Turkey Plate, 9¾"d, turkey gobbler with hen on beige and blue background, artist signed, "Melo." Latrille Mark 1 in green and Straus Mark in red.

PLATE 127

PLATE 129

PLATE 128

PLATE 130

PLATE 127: Rabbit Plate, 8½"d, one of a pair, artist signed, "DuBois." Laviolette Mark in green and Flambeau China Mark 2 in red.

PLATE 128: Rabbit Plate matching one in preceding picture; rabbit hopping across grass.

PLATE 129: Rabbit Plate, 9¼"d, rabbit and dog decoration with scenic wooded background in center of plate extending into border which has a light pink glaze. Theodore Haviland Mark 23 in red, no white ware mark.

PLATE 130: Rabbit Plate, 10"d, rabbits eating carrots, artist signed, "L. Coudert." Borgfeldt Mark 1 in green, no white ware mark.

Cherubs

PLATE 131: Vase, 9"h, large ornate handles decorated in gold; two cherubs holding a dove on matte pink background, outlined with floral and scroll designs in gold. A. Klingenberg Marks 5 in green and 4 in red.

PLATE 132: Biscuit Jar, 7½"h, pair of cherubs holding a white dove on matte pink background gold, sponged trim. (Note that this transfer is the same as the one in preceding picture). Coiffe Mark 2 in green and Bawo & Dotter Mark 11 in red.

PLATE 133

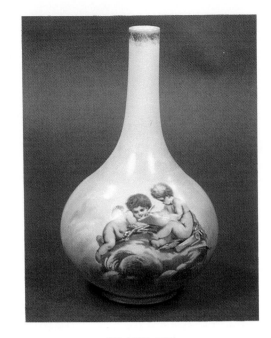

PLATE 135

PLATE 134

PLATE 136

PLATE 133: Charger, 17"x15½", leaf shaped handles painted gold; pair of cherubs decorate center with small multi-colored flowers scattered over surface, brushed gold work on outer border. T&V Mark 7 in green and Leonard Mark in red.

PLATE 134: Vase, 7"h, handled with highly cut footed base; cherub figural with floral garland on pink background; gold trim and enamelled work. Redon Mark 1 in green and Bawo & Dotter Mark 8 in red.

PLATE 135: Vase, 8½"h, two cherubs, one writing while the other watches; pale gray background, brushed gold trim on neck. Redon Mark 1 in green and C. Ahrenfeldt Mark in red.

PLATE 136: Cherub Plate, 9½"d, pair of cupids, one has bow and arrow while the other holds a tablet, pale pink-beige background, gold inner border. T&V Mark 5b in green, no decorating mark, but decoration is French.

PLATE 137: Plate, 10"d, heavily scalloped border forming ornate handles; center decoration of cherubs framed with gold and white flowers. Granger Mark 2 in green, no decorating mark, but work is from a professional French studio.

PLATE 138: Cherub Plate, 8¾"d, cherub in clouds, gold stencilled designs on outer border. Redon Marks 2 in green and 3 in red.

PLATE 139: Cherub Plate, 9"d, cherub holding flower; gold stencilled designs around border. D&CO. Mark 4 in red, no white ware mark.

71

Figural and Floral Cameos

PLATE 140: Biscuit Jar, 8"h, cameo figural decor of couple in eighteenth century dress, framed by gold scroll work with red flowers and green leaves scattered over surface. Laviolette Mark in green and Straus Mark in green.

PLATE 141: Bowl, 10"x 9", deeply scalloped with shell designs on border; cameo figural children decor mixed with scattered floral designs, gold trim. Coiffe Mark 2 in green, no decorating mark, but decoration is French.

PLATE 142: Charger, 15"x12", fancy scalloped border forms handles, center decorated with a figural cameo design of children, heavy gold trim. A. Klingenberg Mark 9 in red, no white ware mark.

PLATE 143: Tray, 10"sq., deeply scalloped and beaded border decorated in gold, orange flowers scattered over body; gold enamelled scroll work frames a cameo of flowers. Granger Mark 2 in green and Straus Mark in gray.

PLATE 144: Charger, 12½"d, scrolled border design forms handles; lavender and white floral reserve decorates center; fancy gold enamelling and trim enhances the tinted pink and cream background. Granger Mark 2 in green and Straus Mark in blue.

Delicate Floral Designs

PLATE 145

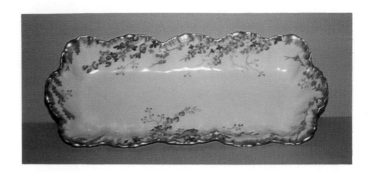

PLATE 146

PLATE 147a

PLATE 147b

PLATE 145: Plate, 8½"d, tiny pink and white floral sprays scattered over surface, gold trim. A. Klingenberg Mark 8 in green and Mark 1 in red,

PLATE 146: Celery Tray, 12"l, 5"w, scalloped and fluted border decorated in gold; dainty multi-colored floral sprays around inner border on pale to dark pink background. Lanternier Mark 4 in green and Leonard Mark in red.

PLATE 147a: Plate, 8"d, small purple flowers decorate left side of plate with enamelled gold leaves and scroll designs on tinted pink background. Straus Mark in gray, no white ware mark.

PLATE 147b: Divided Dish with 3 sections, 11½"x12", with one scrolled handle; gold paste flowers and small light pink roses decorate inner border with pompadour rose glaze on outer border, gold trim. Maas Mark in red, no white ware mark.

PLATE 148

PLATE 149

PLATE 150

PLATE 151

PLATE 148: Cup and Saucer, double ring shaped handle; small yellow and pink flowers and buds with gold paste leaves on pale pink background. Bawo & Dotter Mark 6 in red, no white ware mark.

PLATE 149: Cup and Saucer, bright multi-colored leaves and thistles decorate top of saucer and top portion of cup; lower section of cup finished in pink with gold stippled band and tiny gold flowers. Bawo & Dotter Mark 1 in green, no white ware mark.

PLATE 150: Cup and Saucer, small pink floral reserves, gold enamelled work, bright blue finish. Coiffe Mark 2 in green and Straus Mark in blue.

PLATE 151: Demi-tasse Mustache Cup, gold enamelled floral decor. A. Klingenberg Mark 1 in red.

PLATE 152

PLATE 153

PLATE 154

PLATE 155

PLATE 152: Plate, 9½"d, scalloped and fluted rim; a circle of pink roses decorates center on white body, inner border tinted green and edged with rose garlands, gold outer border. Coiffe Mark 2 in green and Borgfeldt Mark 1 in green.

PLATE 153: Charger, 12½"d, octagon shape, small dark red flowers with light blue-green leaves and tree branches decorate surface. A wide blue band across the top part adds an unusual design. Laviolette Mark in green and Leonard Mark in blue.

PLATE 154: Plate, 8¾"d, dainty multi-colored flowers decorate center and borders, overlaid with gold enamelled work. Martin Marks 1 in green and 3 in blue.

PLATE 155: Plate, 8½"d, a small rose spray in the center of the plate is surrounded by a floral garland, gold trim accents outer border. Coiffe Mark 2 in green and LBH Mark in red.

PLATE 156

PLATE 157

PLATE 158

PLATE 159

PLATE 160

PLATE 161

PLATE 156: Creamer and Sugar, dainty floral sprays, heavy gold trim on scalloped borders, handle, and finial. Laviolette Mark in green and C.J. Ahrenfeldt Mark 1 in blue.

PLATE 157: Mayonnaise Bowl and attached Underplate, a chain of pink flowers encircles middle of bowl, gold trim. Coiffe Mark 2 in green and B&H Mark in gray.

PLATE 158: Fruit Bowl, 10½"d, garlands of pink roses decorate outer border, gold stencilled inner border, small floral clusters in center, gold trim. B&H Mark in red, no white ware mark.

PLATE 159: Tray or Underplate, 12½"d, matches Fruit Bowl in preceding photograph.

PLATE 160: Charger, 12"d, deeply scalloped rim, small violet flowers scattered around outer border and in center, gold trim. Bawo & Dotter Mark 8 in red, no white ware mark.

PLATE 161: Plate, 9"d, lavender and yellow floral sprays scattered across body, gold trim. Vultury Mark in green and B&H Mark in green.

PLATE 162a: Vase (or Letter Holder), 5¾"h, footed, violet flowers and white daisies, some enamelled work, gold trim, artist signed, "Ragoll." Redon Mark 2 in green and Bawo & Dotter Mark 7 in red.

PLATE 162b: Ferner (with liner), 4½"h, 7"d, three ornately scalloped gilded feet; top half decorated with small enamelled flowers on wide light green border divided into sections by darker green triangular shapes. Limoges, France Mark 6 in green and B&H Mark in red.

PLATE 163

PLATE 164

PLATE 165

PLATE 166

PLATE 163: Vase (or Letter Holder), 6½"h, footed, large orange dahlias, green leaves on matte beige background, brushed gold work on body and border. Redon Mark 1 in green, no decorating mark, but decoration is of French origin.

PLATE 164: Vase, 6"h, pedestal base, applied handles, purple flowers with green leaves on matte cream body, gold trim. Gibus and Redon Mark 1 incised and Mark 2 in red.

PLATE 165: Vase, 5⅜" x 4⅝", small bouquets of multi-colored flowers scattered over bulbous body, top of piece has irregular border finished in deep blue; elaborate gold enamelled designs and gold paste flowers over center, lower part of body has pale pink finish, gold trim. Vultury Mark in green and B&H Mark in red.

PLATE 166: Vase, 8½"h, applied handles, short pedestal base, large pink flowers with green leaves on matte white body, gold brush work on base and neck, handles heavily gilded. Redon Mark 2 in green, no decorating mark, but art is of French origin.

PLATE 167: Tea Set: Tray, 16"x13", Creamer, Covered Sugar, Teapot; multi-colored flowers decorate body in spray designs, gold trim. Bawo & Dotter Mark 3 in red, no white ware mark.

PLATE 168: Tea Set: Tray, 21"l, 14"w, Covered Sugar Bowl, Creamer, 3 Cups and Saucers, scalloped and fluted border decorated in gold with pink and green floral clusters scattered across surface. GDA Mark 1 in green, no decorating mark, but decoration is French.

PLATE 169: Chocolate Set: Pot, 13"h, set of 4 Cups and Saucers; fancy scalloped handles and finial decorated in gold, small pink blossoms decorate surface. Limoges, France Mark 4 in green and Borgfeldt Mark 1 in green.

PLATE 170: Pitcher, 8"h, bamboo shaped handle, spray of multi-colored flowers and leaves simply decorate front of pitcher. D&CO. Mark 1 in green, no decorating mark, but art is of French origin.

PLATE 171: Chocolate Pot, 8½"h, applied shell shapes on finial and top of handle decorated in gold, pale lavender floral sprays, green leaves, scalloped base. Leonard Mark in red, no white ware mark.

PLATE 172: Coffee Pot, 10"d, small purple and blue flowers form a floral branch on body and lid, gold trim on spout and twisted finial. Gutherz Mark in red, no white ware mark.

PLATE 173: Cake Plate, 11"d, small multi-colored floral design in center with bird; flowers, bird, and butterfly scattered around outer border, gold trim. H&CO. Mark 12 in green and Frank Haviland Mark 2 in red.

PLATE 174: Dresser Tray, 10½"l, bird perched on floral branch, gold trim, some enamelled work on flowers. Limoges, France Mark 6 in green and AJCO Mark in blue.

PLATE 175

PLATE 176

PLATE 177

PLATE 178

PLATE 175: Dresser Box, 6"l, oval shape, white roses in Art Nouveau style decorate lid and sides of box, gold trim. Beaux Arts French China Mark.

PLATE 176: Picture Frame, 10"x6½", deeply scalloped border forms feet, gold outlines scroll work around edge of frame; small lavender flowers and green leaves on lower half. Latrille Mark 1 in green and Bawo & Dotter Mark 9 in red.

PLATE 177: Fan Box, 9"x1½", small pink roses in garland style encircle inner borders on lid and base. Bawo & Dotter Marks 5 in green and 8 in red.

PLATE 178: Receiving Card Tray, 10"x3", pierced handles, scalloped rim, gold-beaded border and enamelled gold floral sprays, wide green inner border with gold medallion in center. Limoges, France Mark 6 in green and Blakeman & Henderson Mark in green.

Monochrome and Gold Decorations

PLATE 179: Compote, 4½"h, 9"d, simple rose colored bands, gold trim. Marked "Fabrique Par Haviland & Co. Pour W. Boteler & Bro., Washington," in red, ca. 1850s, no white ware mark.

PLATE 180: Covered Bowl, 12"l, nut finial, dark blue band borders, gold trim. H&CO. Mark 1, no decorating mark, but piece is factory decorated.

PLATE 181: Oyster Plate, 10"d, "Pompadour Rose" glaze applied to border and around each individual section; gold stippled designs form pattern between sections; embossed scrolled designs highlighted in gold. T&V Marks 8 in green and 16 in purple.

PLATE 182

PLATE 183

PLATE 184

PLATE 185

PLATE 186

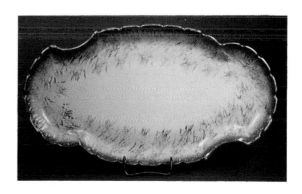

PLATE 187

PLATE 182: Oyster Plates, 6"d, (set of 8), three sections, fluted borders decorated with pale pink glaze, gold trim. GDM Mark 1 in green, no decorating mark, but plates are factory decorated.

PLATE 183: Oyster Plate, 7¾"d, five sections grouped in center of plate; bright blue glaze around sections overlaid with small gold floral designs. H&CO. Mark 9 in green with "Haviland & Co. for Ovington Brothers, Brooklyn" as decorating mark.

PLATE 184: Cup and Saucer, dark brown glaze around borders shading to lighter brown, gold brush work and trim featuring a leaf design on body. Redon Marks 1 in green and 3 in red.

PLATE 185: Cup and Saucer, gold enameled scroll work and tiny flowers on border of each piece. D&CO. Mark 3 in green and B&CO. Mark 3 in red.

PLATE 186: Plate, 9½"d, wine glazed border overlaid with gold leaves. GDM Mark 1 in green, no decorating mark, but art is factory or French studio.

PLATE 187: Receiving Card Tray, 9¼"l, deep rose border, gold spattered designs frame center, gold trim. Redon Mark 2 in green and Leonard Mark in red.

PLATE 188: Jam Jar and Underplate, cobalt blue enamelled finish decorated with gold stencilled designs, heavily gilded handles and finial. Pouyat Marks 5 in green and 9 in pink and green.

PLATE 189: Plate, 6½"d, cobalt blue outer border trimmed with gold stencilled flowers, gold medallion in center. Pouyat Marks 5 in green and 7 in red.

PLATE 190: Tray, 13"l, 8"w, wide cobalt blue border frames center, gold leaves and beaded work on border and handles, pale yellow-gold flowers scattered over center. GDM Mark 1 in green, no decorating mark, but decoration is factory.

PLATE 191: Demi-tasse Cups and Saucers, bamboo shaped handles, decoration in cobalt blue is like that of tray in preceding photograph and is marked the same.

PLATE 192: Bowl, 13"x8", cobalt blue, similar to pieces in preceding two photographs.

PLATE 193

PLATE 194

PLATE 195

PLATE 196

PLATE 193: Chocolate Pot, 9"h, gold paste floral designs on white body. Coiffe Mark 2 in green and Bawo & Dotter Mark 6 in red.

PLATE 194: Oyster Plate, 7½"d, five sections, soft cream finish with brushed gold work on borders and center of plate. Lanternier Mark 2 in green and C. Ahrenfeldt Mark in red.

PLATE 195: Bowl, 12½"d, scalloped and fluted border heavily decorated in gold; gold stencilled medallion in center. Laviolette Mark in green and Leonard Mark in blue.

PLATE 196: Cake Plate, 10"d, scalloped border with beaded work finished in gold; gold medallion in center, cream background. Limoges, France Mark 1 in green and A. Klingenberg mark in red.

PLATE 197: Plate with Cup and Saucer decorated with simple gold bands (wedding ring design). Charles Field Haviland Mark 2 in green, no decorating mark, but pieces are factory decorated.

PLATE 198: Covered Sugar Bowl, 8¼"h and Creamer, 6"h, matching gold band decorated pieces in preceding photograph.

PLATE 199: Coffee Pot, 9"h, part of set featured in previous two photographs.

PLATE 200

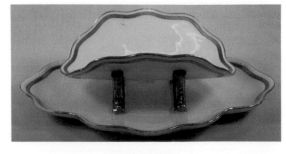

PLATE 203

PLATE 201

PLATE 204

PLATE 202

PLATE 205

PLATE 200: Butter Pat, 3"d, gold band border, T&V Marks 7 in green and 16 in purple.

PLATE 201: Shaving Mug, 3"h, narrow gold band trim. H&CO. Marks 6 in green and 18 in blue.

PLATE 202: Sauce Boat and Underplate, gold trim and gold outlined designs. Frank Haviland Mark 1 in red.

PLATE 203: Asparagus Dish, 9"l, 6"w; Underplate, 13"l, 10"w, scalloped outer borders trimmed in gold with gold band inner borders; applied feet finished in gold. Martin Marks 1 in green and 3 in blue without "Décor" or "Déposé."

PLATE 204: Egg Dish, 9¼"d, gold trim on fluted borders. GDM Marks 1 in green and 3 in brown.

PLATE 205: Platter, 14"l, 8"w, embossed designs on handles and border trimmed in gold. Pouyat Marks 3 in green and 4 in red.

French Decoration–Patterns

The third section of French Decorated Limoges illustrates patterns. The pieces shown are patterns made by the various Limoges factories for table ware items and some small decorative accessories. Generally these pieces and their patterns were made to be used, in contrast to the plates and other table ware pieces designed for display as shown in the previous section. The patterns are transfers, although some pieces may have some enamelled work, and nearly all have gold trim.

The first part of this section features several pieces in the Moss Rose pattern, one of the early and popular Limoges patterns. A selection of pieces decorated with rich and bold transfer patterns follows. These represent the Limoges image through their vibrant and unique patterns. A series of game bird plates and a few other patterns made by Haviland & Co. are also shown as examples which are exceptions to the general Haviland image of dainty floral patterns.

Oyster plates are shown at the end of the first part of this section. These are a specialized area of collecting, and examples can be found in a number of patterns. While many are highly decorative, most seemed to have been designed for use. Totally handpainted examples are rare, in contrast to fish and game sets pictured in the previous section. Some of the more vividly decorated ones precede the other floral patterns which serve as a transition to the second part of this section. (Also see a few oyster plates at the end of Section 2.)

Table ware patterns decorated with delicate floral transfer designs complete the section on Limoges patterns. Age and object may form the basis for collecting some of these pieces rather than their unique decoration. There are exceptions, of course, such as "Old Blackberry" which is a popular and very collectible Haviland pattern.

Some of the pieces in this section are examples of a rare or scarce mark. Items such as pitchers, chocolate pots, butter pats, and cups and saucers can form attractive collections based on different patterns of the same object or the same pattern for different objects. Unusual pieces such as cheese dishes, ice cream or pudding sets, and pancake dishes are collectible because of their scarcity. Some other items besides table wares are included here because of their transfer decoration, such as desk and dresser items.

Very few Limoges patterns have "names" stamped on them, and I have not tried to devise names for patterns or identify any Haviland pattern unless it is commonly known. While a number of patterns are shown, this book is not designed to be a pattern matching book. The emphasis is on decoration, marks, and objects with a view to collecting.

Moss Rose Pattern

PLATE 206: Vase, 7½"h, square shape, knob feet, Moss Rose pattern. H&CO. Mark 16 in blue with "Pour Glover Harrison Toronto."

PLATE 207: Chamber Stick, applied ring handle, Moss Rose decor, blue trim. H&CO. Mark 16 in blue with "Pour Glover Harrison Toronto."

PLATE 208: Soap Dish, 4½"l, pierced lid, Moss Rose design, gold trim. H&CO. Mark 9 in green and Mark 18 in blue.

PLATE 209

PLATE 210

PLATE 211

PLATE 212

PLATE 209: Soup Bowl, 9½"d, Moss Rose in center of bowl, gold trim. H&CO. Mark 9 in green, no decorating mark, but piece is factory decorated.

PLATE 210: Cream Pitcher, 5½"h, elegantly curved handle with embossed leaf and flower designs on body outlined in gold; Moss Rose pattern decorates body and lid. AV Mark impressed.

PLATE 211: Coffee Pot, 10"h, matches Cream Pitcher in preceding photograph.

PLATE 212: Sugar Bowl, 7½"h, molded rope design on finial and handles, Moss Rose decoration, blue trim. H&CO. Mark 5 impressed and Mark 9 in green, factory decoration.

PLATE 213: Tea Tile, 6½"d, Moss Rose pattern. Charles Field Haviland Mark 3 in black, no white ware mark.

PLATE 214: Bowl, 12"l, oblong shape with one pierced handle; Moss Rose pattern around inner border with blue-gray band, gold trim on embossed designs around handles. Charles Field Haviland Mark 1 impressed, factory decoration.

PLATE 215: Platter, 12½"l, matches Bowl in preceding photograph.

Bold and Unusual Patterns

PLATE 216: Plate, 7½"d, "Flow Blue" type floral design, gold trim. Pouyat Marks 3 in green and 6 in red.

PLATE 217: Covered Vegetable Dish, 11"l, 6"h, "Flow Blue" type pattern, gold trim. GDM Mark 2 in green and E.G.D. & Co. Mark in green.

PLATE 218: Platter, 12"l, matches Dish in preceding photograph.

PLATE 219

PLATE 220

PLATE 221

PLATE 222

PLATE 219: Compote, 9¼"d, 2½"h, pink, lavender, and orange flowers scattered over surface, brushed gold on scallops around border. D&CO. Marks 3 in green and 6 in red.

PLATE 220: Fruit Bowl, 11"d, pedestal base, blue-green border overlaid with small pink roses and green leaves in garland designs decorate interior and exterior of bowl, gold trim. H&CO. Marks 12 in green and 13 in gold.

PLATE 221: Punch Bowl, 9½"d, 4½"h, Large white and pink enamelled blossoms on interior and exterior of bowl; deep green glaze on exterior, gold trim. T&V Marks 6 in green and 10 in red.

PLATE 222: Centerpiece Bowl, 9"d, 2½"h with Underplate, 14"d, elaborate mold composed of three section scallops around top and base; pink, yellow, and blue floral garlands with small scattered flowers, beaded gold work on interior of scallops, gold trim. H&CO. Marks 12 in green and 13 in red.

PLATE 223: Pitcher, 11"h, large pink flowers scattered over body, heavily gilded handle and top border. Pouyat Marks 5 in green and 9 in pink and green.

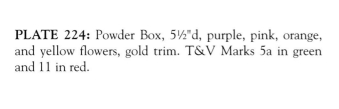

PLATE 224: Powder Box, 5½"d, purple, pink, orange, and yellow flowers, gold trim. T&V Marks 5a in green and 11 in red.

PLATE 225: Dresser Set: Pair of Candle Holders, 6"h, Powder Box, Ring Tray, 2 cologne Bottles, 4"h with stoppers; bright red-orange and purple flowers with deep pink finish shading to white. GDM Mark 2 in green, no decorator mark, but decoration is French.

PLATE 226: Candle Holders, 6"h, maroon, pink, and yellow roses, gold brushed work on base. T&V Marks 8 in green and 16 in purple.

PLATE 227

PLATE 228

PLATE 229

PLATE 230

PLATE 227: Coffee Pot, 11"h, multi-colored geometric designs in an Art Deco fashion form top border of pot and base of lid, gold spout and handle. J. Boyer Marks 1 in green and 2 in blue.

PLATE 228: Demi-tasse Cup and Saucer, attached shell-shaped handle decorated in gold; autumn colored flowers on body, gold trim. GDM Marks 1 in green and 3 in blue.

PLATE 229: Chocolate Pot, 10"h, large orange flowers compose borders with a few flowers on lower part of pot, heavy gold finish on handle and finial. Pouyat Marks 5 in green and 9 in pink and green.

PLATE 230: Mug, 5½"h, reserves of pink roses on each side framed with gold scroll designs, gold trim. T&V Marks 7 in green and 16 in purple.

PLATE 231

PLATE 233

PLATE 232

PLATE 234

PLATE 231: Cracker Jar, 6"h, 8"w and Underplate, 8¼"d, large pink roses with green leaves, gold trim. T&V Marks 7 in green and 11 in red.

PLATE 232: Plate, 10"d, floral garlands, cameos, and ribbons form outer border pattern; blue inner border overlaid with gold floral pattern, gold trim. Guérin Mark 3 in green and Bawo & Dotter Mark 12 in black and brown.

PLATE 233: Dresser Tray, 12½"l, 8½"w, scrolled border forms handles, large white enamelled daisies on tinted orange background encircle inside of tray with one daisy in center, gold trim. T&V marks 8 in green and 16 in purple.

PLATE 234: Cake Plate, 10¾"d, Dresden type floral bouquets decorate center and border, gold trim. Theodore Haviland Mark 35 in red with Mark 29 enclosed in a square with "Ivory China" in green and the pattern name "Dubarry."

PLATE 235: Game Bird Plates, 9"d, transfers of small game birds in light brown tones decorate surface, overlapping borders and forming design around the outer edge of the plate. The set has the same type decor with three different colors of borders (see following 2 pictures); yellow border shown here. H&CO. Marks 10 in green and 17 in red.

PLATE 236: Game Bird Plate with wine border.

PLATE 237: Game Bird Plate with blue border.

PLATE 238

PLATE 239

PLATE 240

PLATE 241

PLATE 238: Plate, 9½" sq., Napkin Fold edge, brown monochrome scenic decoration of hunter in woods with raccoon in tree. H&CO. Marks 9 in green and 17 in brown.

PLATE 239: Plate, 9"d, birds and butterfly pattern, gold stencilled border design. H&CO. Marks 8 in green and 16 in blue with "Davis Collamore & Co. New York."

PLATE 240: Game Bird Plate, 9½"d, pair of birds in brush. H&CO. Mark 9 in green, made for the Tynedale Company in Philadelphia.

PLATE 241: Plate, 8"d, Oriental scenic and figural design. H&CO. Marks 12 in green and 13 in red, noted as being decorated for Jenner & Co., Edinburgh.

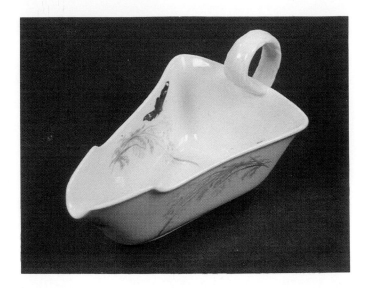

PLATE 242: Sauce Boat, 7"l, butterflies and floral branches, a Haviland pattern now popularly referred to as "Meadow Visitors." H&CO. Mark 17 in black with an English registry mark.

PLATE 243: Tea Pot, 6"l, basket-weave mold, bird, butterfly, and leaf design (Meadow Visitors). H&CO. Marks 8 in green and 18 in blue.

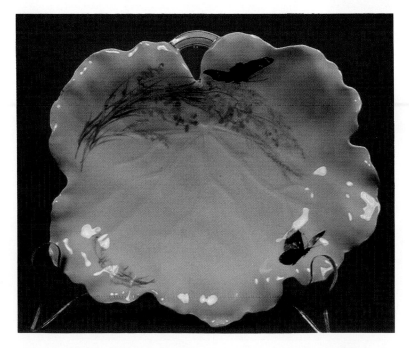

PLATE 244: Leaf Dish, 8¼"d, Meadow Visitors pattern. H&CO. Marks 8 in green and 17 in green.

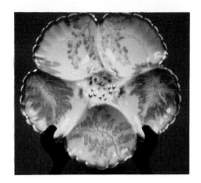

PLATE 245

PLATE 246

PLATE 247

PLATE 248

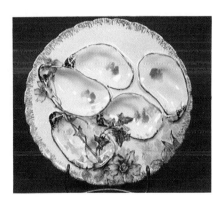

PLATE 249

PLATE 250

PLATE 245: Oyster Plate, 8"d, 5 sections decorated with leaf designs, beaded work in center, brushed gold border. T&V Marks 8 in green and 16 in purple.

PLATE 246: Oyster Plate, 6"d, 3 sections, fluted border brushed with gold, large blue flowers. GDM Marks 1 in green and 3 in black.

PLATE 247: Oyster Plate, 9"d, pentagon shape, 5 sections with center sauce dip; gold, red, green, and black designs form pattern around inner border, gold trim. Bawo & Dotter Marks 5 in green and 9 in red (without "Handpainted").

PLATE 248: Oyster Plate, 9"d, 6 sections with center sauce dip; large violet flowers decorate each section, gold trim. Illegible white ware mark with A. Klingenberg Mark 2 in red.

PLATE 249: Oyster Plate, 7¾"d, 5 shell shaped sections arranged across center of plate; large pink flowers, short vertical lines in gold around border. H&CO. Marks 9 in green and 13 in red.

PLATE 250: Oyster Plate, 8½"d, individual sections formed by lightly scrolled scalloped shapes; wide gold border overlaid with blue enamelled floral and scroll work, gold stencilled medallion in center. Coiffe Mark 2 in green and Straus Mark in blue.

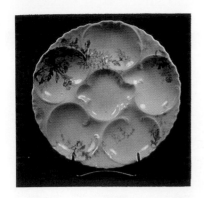

PLATE 251

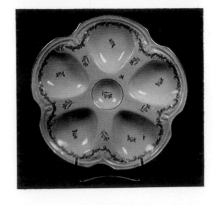

PLATE 252

PLATE 253

PLATE 254

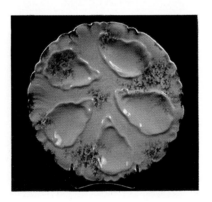

PLATE 255

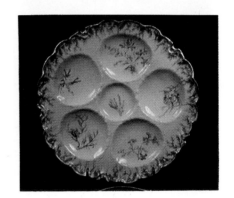

PLATE 256

PLATE 251: Oyster Plate, 8¼"d, 5 sections with center sauce dip, pale pink flowers highlighted by gray foliage. H&CO. Marks 11 in green and 13 in red.

PLATE 252: Oyster Plate, 8½"d, 5 sections with center sauce dip; a small pink rose decorates each section with a small blue flower separating sections, gold trim. Coiffe Mark 3 in green with Demartine Mark 2 in green.

PLATE 253: Oyster Plate, 8¼"d, 5 sections and sauce dip formed by large scrolled designs; small yellow and pink flowers with gray foliage scattered over surface. H&CO. Marks 11 in green and 13 in red.

PLATE 254: Oyster Plate, 8¼"d, 5 sections, center sauce dip brushed with gold; small pink rose garlands around outer border, gold brushed work on outer edges. Theodore Haviland Mark 33 in red.

PLATE 255: Oyster Plate, 8¾"d, 5 shell shaped sections; large lavender flowers form irregular pattern on surface with edges brushed with gold. GDA Marks 1 in green and 3 in red.

PLATE 256: Oyster Plate, 9"d, 5 sections with center sauce dip; pale pink and lavender floral sprays with green leaves decorate inner border and body, gold trim. H&CO. Marks 12 in green and 13 in red for "D.B. Bedell & Co., Fifth Avenue, New York."

PLATE 257

PLATE 258

PLATE 259

PLATE 257: Pitcher, 9"h, scalloped rim, heavily scrolled handle and base ("Richelieu" form), highlighted with gold; yellow-orange flowers and green leaves lightly scattered over body. H&CO. Marks 9 in green and 13 in red.

PLATE 258: Pitcher, 4½"h, pink floral spray descending from top of pitcher, gold trim. H&CO. Marks 9 in green and 13 in red.

PLATE 259: Pitcher, 9"h, with ice lip; yellow flowers, gold trim on handle. GDM Mark 1 in green, factory decoration.

PLATE 260

PLATE 261

PLATE 262

PLATE 263

PLATE 260: Chocolate Pot, 6½"h, small pink flowers form borders on lid and around top and base of pot with a few scattered around middle of body, gold trim. GDA Marks 1 in green and 3 in red with Haviland and Abbot Mark in red.

PLATE 261: Chocolate Pot, 10"h, "Q" shaped handle and finial, scalloped base; pink floral pattern, gold trim and gold spattered work on handle and finial. Martin Marks 1 in green and 3 in blue.

PLATE 262: Chocolate Pot, 10½"h, pink rose cameos decorate lid and form border around top, gold trim. D&CO. Mark 3 in green and B&CO. Mark 3 in red.

PLATE 263: Chocolate Pot, 9½"h, clusters of pink roses between fancy gold stencilled designs decorate upper part of pot and lid, gold trim. D&CO. Mark 3 in green and B&CO. Mark 3 in red.

PLATE 264: Coffee Pot, 11"h, double ring shaped handle and finial, sprays of large blue flowers serve as pattern with gold leaves at base of spout. GDA Marks 1 in green and 3 in red.

PLATE 265: Chocolate Pot, 11"h, same form as Coffee Pot in previous photograph with handle and finial finished in gold. GDM Mark 2 in green, no decorating mark, but piece is factory decorated.

PLATE 266

PLATE 267

PLATE 269

PLATE 268

PLATE 270

PLATE 266: Cup and Saucer, pink floral garlands, gold trim. Borgfeldt Mark 1 in green, no white ware mark.

PLATE 267: Covered Bouillon Cup and Mug, 3"h, both fashioned with Egyptian motif handles and finial, "Isis" design, each decorated with pastel floral designs and gold trim. Bouillon Cup has GDM Marks 1 in green and 3 in blue; Mug has GDM Marks 2 in green and 3 in brown.

PLATE 268: Coffee Cup, 5"d and Saucer, 6½"d, large size for *café au lait*; blue floral sprays, handle brushed with gold. Theodore Haviland Mark 32 in red.

PLATE 269: Cup and Saucer, simply decorated with pale pink flowers and brushed gold. Laporte Mark 2 in red.

PLATE 270: Cup and Saucer, pink and yellow roses, gray foliage, gold trim. J. MC. D. & S. Mark 2 in red, no white ware mark.

PLATE 271: Shaving Mug, 3¼"h, large pink roses and green leaves. H&CO. Marks 8 in green and 17 in brown.

PLATE 272: Demi-tasse Cup and Saucer, yellow geometric designs around inner border, gold trim. Balleroy Mark 1 in green and Florale Mark in green.

PLATE 273: Demi-tasse Cup and Saucer, blue flowers, brushed gold trim. H&CO. Marks 11 in green and 13 in red.

PLATE 274

PLATE 275

PLATE 276

PLATE 277

PLATE 274: Toast Tray, 7½"l, dainty blue and green flowers, gold trim. A. Klingenberg Marks 7 in green and 9 in red.

PLATE 275: Pancake Dish, 10"d, pierced lid, small blue flowers on long stems, gold trim. GDM Marks 2 in green and 3 in brown.

PLATE 276: Grapefruit Dish, 2"h, 4½"d, attached underplate; green and wine geometric designs form simple border pattern with wine outer border on underplate. Theodore Haviland Mark 34 in red.

PLATE 277: Waste Bowl, 5"d, pink roses, brushed gold border. Latrille Mark 2 in red, no white ware mark.

PLATE 278

PLATE 279

PLATE 280

PLATE 281

PLATE 282

PLATE 283

PLATE 278: Ice Cream Bowl, 7"l, pink and gray floral sprays, gold trim on handle. H&CO. Marks 12 in green and 13 in red.

PLATE 279: Hors d'oeuvre Plate, 6"l, fancy scalloped shape, multi-colored flowers around border extending toward center, brushed gold around edge. H&CO. Marks 11 in green and 13 in red.

PLATE 280: Berry Dish, 5"d, 3 different floral designs form simple pattern around inner border into center with outer border trimmed in green. H&CO. Marks 8 in green and 17 in black.

PLATE 281: Salt Dip, 2¾"d, small white and violet blossoms, brushed gold trim, GDM Marks 2 in green and 3 in brown.

PLATE 282: Berry Bowl, 5¼"d, red-orange flowers with green leaves, gold trim. Demartine Mark 1 in green and J. MC. D. & S. Mark 1 in red.

PLATE 283: Basket, 7½"l, pierced on top with hole on the side for discarding water or juice, basket weave design on body and handle; multi-colored flowers. H&CO. Marks 8 in green and 18 in blue.

PLATE 284: Butter Pat, 3¼"d, embossed scalloped rim with beaded work; pale green and yellow flowers. Bassett Mark in red, no white ware mark.

PLATE 285: Mayonnaise Dish and Underplate, leaf shape, large pink roses with green leaves, gold trim. H&CO. Marks 12 in green and 13 in red with "For E.H. Murray, Watertown, New York."

PLATE 286: Mayonnaise Dish and Underplate, leaf shape similar to one in preceding picture; pale pink roses, brushed gold on edges. H&CO. Marks 12 in green and 13 in red with "For Leighton Bros., Lowell, Mass."

PLATE 287

PLATE 288

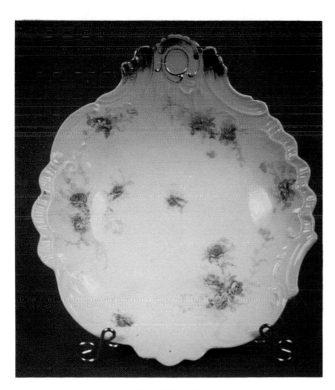

PLATE 289

PLATE 290

PLATE 287: Bowl, 10"l, one handle formed from ornately scalloped border, decorated with a pattern of small violet flowers, brushed gold work on handle. Pouyat Marks 5 in green and 7 in red.

PLATE 288: Bowl, 9¼" d, one open handle decorated in gold; large pink roses and green leaves around inner border, gold trim. H&CO. Marks 12 in green and 13 in red.

PLATE 289: Bowl, 10"l, same shape as one above with a different pattern of pink roses. Pouyat Marks 5 in green and 7 in red.

PLATE 290: Bowl, 6"l, shaped with one handle; blue flowers, gold outlining on handle and part of border. GDM Marks 1 in green and 3 in red.

PLATE 291

PLATE 292

PLATE 293

PLATE 294

PLATE 295

PLATE 296

PLATE 291: Basket, 6"l, scalloped border with split handle; small blue flowers, brushed gold on handle. Lanternier Marks 3 in green and 6 in brown.

PLATE 292: Cheese Dish, 7"h, Underplate, 8¼"sq , finial shaped in Egyptian "Isis" style; scattered yellow flowers. GDM Marks 1 in green and 3 in black

PLATE 293: Open Vegetable Bowl, 9¾"l, 7½"w, beaded work on handles; yellow inner border with small red and white floral designs, gold trim. Vignaud Marks 3 in green and 2 in green.

PLATE 294: Strawberry Bowl (with drain) and Underplate, 7½"d, pierced serving bowl; pink and white floral pattern, gold trim. Bawo & Dotter Marks 5 in green and 9 in red.

PLATE 295: Bowl, 3¾"sq, pedestal base, "Old Blackberry" pattern. H&CO. Marks 9 in green and 18 in blue-green.

PLATE 296: Basket, 10"l, woven handle; pale to dark blue-gray flowers and leaves form interior pattern. H&CO. Marks 8 in green and 18 in blue-green.

PLATE 297

PLATE 298

PLATE 299

PLATE 300

PLATE 297: Plate, 7"d, blue and gold chain design interspersed with small pink flowers and green leaves, gold trim. Créange Marks 1 in green and 2 in black and gold.

PLATE 298: Plate, 10"d, "Autumn Leaf" pattern. H&CO. Marks 12 in green and 13 in red.

PLATE 299: Tureen, 13"l, 7"h, deeply scalloped handles and finial lightly brushed with gold; pink, blue, and gray floral pattern. Guérin Marks 2 in green and 4 in red.

PLATE 300: Plate, 9¼"d, gold stencilled center medallion, green and gold geometric design with small flowers around inner border, gold trim. CMC Mark in green and Levy (Imperial) Mark in red.

PLATE 301: Cake Plate, 11"d, double pierced handles; delicate pink and white flowers scattered over surface, brushed gold on border. Pouyat Marks 5 in green and 8 in green.

PLATE 302: Cake Plate, 10½"d, green and red geometric pattern on outer border with similar medallions scattered around inner border, gold trim. GDA Marks 1 in green and 3 in red.

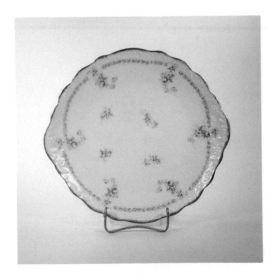

PLATE 303: Cake Plate, 10½"d, embossed floral designs around border, small pink roses encircle inner border and are scattered over surface. A&D Mark in green, no white ware mark.

PLATE 304

PLATE 305

PLATE 306a

PLATE 307

PLATE 306b

PLATE 304: Pudding Bowl, 9"d, orange flowers with green leaves and blue background flowers, gold trim. Coiffe Mark 2 in green and Bawo & Dotter Mark 8 in red.

PLATE 305: Gravy Boat, 7½"l and Underplate, 9¼"l, scrolled handle; small pink, yellow and blue flowers, enamelled, form border pattern, gold trim. GDM Marks 1 in green and 3 in blue.

PLATE 306a: Pudding Set: Serving Bowl, 9½"d, Baking Liner, 7"d, Underplate, 11"d; tinted pink inner border with small pink roses forming garland around center and

scattered in middle of Underplate; scrolled edges undecorated except for small touches of gold. T&V Marks 5a in green and 11 in red.

PLATE 306b: Charger, 11½"d, same mold design as Pudding Set with similar decoration except inner border is tinted green. T&V Marks 5a in green and 11 in red.

PLATE 307: Punch Bowl, 6¼"h, 14"d on a 3"h separate base, same pattern and mold as Plate 306b; 8 matching punch cups. T&V Marks 8 in green and 16 in purple.

119

PLATE 308

PLATE 310

PLATE 311

PLATE 309

PLATE 312

PLATE 308: Charger, 11½"d, same mold design as Plate 306b with a different decoration; large white daisies around inner border with outer border painted gold. T&V Marks 8 in green and 16 in purple.

PLATE 309: Baking dish, 12"d, scallop shell shaped handles painted gold, small pink flowers, brushed gold border. CFH Mark 4, no decorating mark but piece is factory decorated.

PLATE 310: Platter, 17½"l, small pink roses around inner border and in center, gold trim on handles. Guérin Marks 3 in green and 3 in blue.

PLATE 311: Platter, 13½"l, pink blossoms form irregular pattern on body, embossed designs on handles outlined in gold. H&CO. Marks 12 in green and 13 in red.

PLATE 312: Chamber Stick, 3½"h, simple leaf design around inner border, gold trim. GDA Marks 1 in green and 3 in red.

PLATE 313

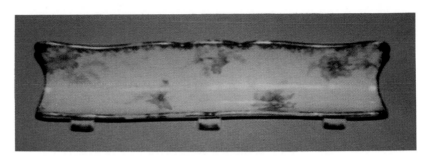

PLATE 314

PLATE 315

PLATE 316

PLATE 313: Bonbon Dish, 6"x4½", pierced handle, pink roses, brushed gold trim. GDM Mark 1 in green, no decorating mark, but piece is factory decorated.

PLATE 314: Pen Tray, 6"l, footed, yellow flowers, brushed gold trim. GDM Mark 2 in green, no decorating mark, but piece is factory decorated.

PLATE 315: Match Box with striker in top of lid; pale floral pattern, brushed gold border, GDA Mark 1 in green, factory decorated.

PLATE 316: Dresser Tray, 13½"l, irregular scalloped edge, autumn colored floral garlands around interior border. LR&L Mark 1 in red, no white ware mark.

PLATE 317: Dresser tray, 12"l, fluted edge, pale pink-beige flowers accented with gray leaves. H&CO. Marks 12 in green and 13 in red.

PLATE 317

Specialty and Unusual Items

      This fourth section of French decorated Limoges includes neither art objects nor patterns. These pieces are collectible because of rarity or specialized collecting interest. Examples of table china in animal form designed by the artist Sandoz and made by the Theodore Haviland Company during the Art Deco era are highly collectible.

      Salesman's samples from the Haviland Company represent scarce and unusual Limoges items as do table lamps and a doll. A few advertising items for cognac are also shown. Very few advertising pieces appear to have been made by the Limoges factories. Souvenir pieces are more easily found, but they also occupy a rather scarce category of collectible Limoges. A set of plates made for the 1900 Paris Exhibition is shown here as well a box depicting the Eiffel Tower. One example of hotel china is also included which represents another specialized collecting category.

PLATE 318: Salt and Pepper Shakers in frog shape designed by Sandoz and made by the Theodore Haviland Company, artist signed. Theodore Haviland Marks 29 in green and 34 in red.

PLATE 319: Pitcher, 7"h, Penquin design by Sandoz, reflecting the Art Deco influence, artist signed. Theodore Haviland Mark 34 in red.

PLATE 320: Souvenir Plates, 9¼"d, three plates commemorating the 1900 Exposition in Paris, transfer designs of different buildings. Pouyat Mark 5 in green, no decorating mark, but decoration was probably by a Paris studio; the first is entitled: *"Exposition Universelle de 1900 Vue General."*

PLATE 321: Souvenir plate entitled: *"Pavillion National des Etats Unis."*

PLATE 322: Souvenir Plate entitled: *"Palais Étrangers."*

PLATE 323: Tea Set: Teapot, 5"h, 7"w; Open Sugar Bowl, 5"h, Creamer, 4½"h; decorated with the United States seal, gold stencilled work on borders, heavily gilded handles. Raynaud Mark 1 in green on tea pot and T&V Mark 9 in green on the sugar and creamer with all marked "The National Remembrance Shop, Washington, D.C." in purple. These pieces were special order souvenir items from the Raynaud factory.

PLATE 324: Vase, 7½"h, matches Tea Set with U.S. seal. Raynaud Mark1 in green and "The National Remembrance Shop, Washington, D.C." in purple.

PLATE 325: Pitcher, 8½"h, salesman's sample showing two different decorations for the pitcher; the designs are separated by a wide gold band. H&CO. Mark 8 in green.

PLATE 326: Sandwich Set: Plate, 9"l, salesman's sample, indicated by markings on the back (mark not shown), and H&CO. Mark 11 in green.

PLATE 327

PLATE 328

PLATE 329

PLATE 330

PLATE 327: Ashtray, 4½"d, advertising item for Grand Marnier Cherry Cognac. Union Limousine Mark 8 in green, no decorating mark, but decoration is French.

PLATE 328: Trinket Box, 4¼"d, Souvenir item showing the Eiffel Tower. Fontanille and Marraud Mark 4 in green, factory decoration.

PLATE 329: Tip Tray, 6"l, advertising Hine Cognac. Robert Haviland Mark 2 in black.

PLATE 330: Hotel China, Soup Bowl, 9½"d, brown floral pattern decorates flange of bowl, cream colored body. H&CO. Mark 9 in green, made for the "West Hotel, Minneapolis and St. Paul, Minnesota, 1885."

PLATE 331

PLATE 332

PLATE 333

PLATE 331: Lamp, 9½"h (originally fueled by oil), violets on white background, brushed gold accents on base. D&CO. Mark 3 in green, no decorating mark, but piece is factory decorated.

PLATE 332: Lamp Base, 11"h, cream finish, brass mountings. Theodore Haviland Mark 29 in green.

PLATE 333: Fashion Doll made by Lanternier during the years of World War I.

Undecorated Limoges

Blanks or undecorated Limoges porcelain is a natural transition from French decorated objects to American decorated Limoges. Undecorated Limoges is often a "sleeper." Occasionally, such pieces surface which for some reason failed to get decorated. In some cases, this is good, for the piece may be more collectible than if it had been painted poorly by an amateur.

The details of the mold and workmanship of the potter are very visible on blanks. The vase shown here is just one example, making an exquisite decorative piece on its own. The triangular shaped coffee set and dragon handled tankard are also quite striking, when devoid of decoration.

PLATE 334: Vase, 9½"h, 8"w, elegantly scalloped handles and neck. Pouyat Mark 5 in green.

PLATE 335

PLATE 336

PLATE 337

PLATE 338

PLATE 335: Platter, 14"l, 9½"w, scalloped border forming handles, embossed designs around inner border. Barny & Rigoni Mark 3 in green.

PLATE 336: Wash Basin and Pitcher, six-sided, undecorated. B&CO. Mark 1 in green.

PLATE 337: Tea Pot, 5½"h, 7"w handle to spout, embossed designs on handle extending onto body, undecorated. Pouyat Mark 5 in green.

PLATE 338: Butter Pat, 3½"d, scalloped border. H&CO. Mark 6 in green.

PLATE 339

PLATE 340a

PLATE 340b

PLATE 341

PLATE 339: Talcum Shaker, 5"h, three feet with delicate scroll designs at top. La Porcelaine Limousine Mark 1 in green.

PLATE 340a: Tankard, 14¾"h, scalloped neck, dragon shaped handle. Pouyat Mark 5 in green.

PLATE 340b: Tankard, 10¾"h, undecorated white ware. Pouyat Mark 5 in green.

PLATE 341: Coffee Set: Pot, Covered Sugar, Creamer; triangular shaped mold, braided rope handles and finials, applied rope and knot designs on body, undecorated. H&CO. Mark 9 in green.

American Decorated Limoges

The blanks shown in the preceding section are just a few examples of the numerous types of white wares or undecorated china exported to America by many of the Limoges factories during the late 1800s and early 1900s. This was a lucrative market for the manufacturers because china painting was a hobby for many people and a profession for others. Most American decorated pieces, however, prove that this form of art on Limoges blanks was executed more by amateurs than by professional artists.

This category of decoration is divided into three sections. First are examples of professional decoration. The pieces have only an underglaze white ware mark, however, and the lack or illegibility of a signature makes it impossible to attribute the piece definitely as French decoration. Some very fine paintings on porcelain are illustrated. These are followed by items which were decorated by American art studios, mostly from the Pickard firm.

The second section of American decoration includes pieces which have Quality Decoration. Determining and differentiating such pieces is often a personal judgement. Criteria in choosing include care in painting as well as good choice of color, shading and design.

The third section represents Amateur Decoration. In some cases, the pieces are quite collectible. The large jardinieres and punch bowls as well as many tankards are found in this category. Amateur art is evident, however, when subjects, such as roses, are out of proportion or the background is "cold" painted, or too dark, or does not blend well with the decoration. Uneven borders, very dark backgrounds, pearlized finishes, and superfluous gold work as well as large monogramming are indications of amateur china painters. Signatures placed on the face of an object in very bold letters or with a date, or signed on the bottom are very obvious clues that the painter was a novice. Exceptions to signing on the bottom are artist's small initials without dates, of course. Always examine the gold trim to see that it, as well as any other outlining, has been applied carefully .

Because the photographs in this section are divided by quality of art work, prices in the Price Guide have not been coded. It is apparent from the particular section where the piece is shown whether it is an example of American Professional, Quality, or Amateur decoration. For the same reason, the caption for each of the pictures does not include "American handpainted."

American Professional Decoration

PLATE 342: Painting on porcelain, 8"l, 6"w, framed, figural scene of woman with fishing pole and cherub on river bank. T&V Mark 5a.

PLATE 343

PLATE 344

PLATE 343: Painting on porcelain, 16"d, framed, Lion poised on edge of cliff, artist signed (illegible), matches panting in following photograph.

PLATE 344: Painting on porcelain, 15x12", framed, lion and lioness, artist signed, Pouyat Mark 5 in green.

PLATE 345

PLATE 346

PLATE 345: Painting on porcelain, 14"l, 7"w, figural portraits of two partially nude women surrounded by a wispy drape and clouds, artist signed (illegible), T&V Mark 7 in green.

PLATE 346: Painting on porcelain, 16"l, 14"w, reclining nude figure in an Art Nouveau style. T&V Mark 7 in green.

133

PLATE 347

PLATE 348

PLATE 347: Vase, 14"h, desert scene with camel, artist signed, "Steffin," artist for the Pairpoint Company. Pairpoint Mark in green.

PLATE 348: Vase, 13½"h, red poinsettias on cream colored background with distinctive Pickard gold work, artist signed, "Yeschek." Pouyat Mark 5 in green and a Pickard decorating mark.

PLATE 349: Cachepot, 12"h, 10"w, applied ring shaped handles, knob feet, fruit decor. Guérin Mark 3 in green with a Pickard decorating mark.

PLATE 349

PLATE 350: Plate, 9"d, clusters of grapes around inner border, gold trim, artist signed, "E. Challinor." H&CO. Mark 12 in green and a Pickard decorating mark.

PLATE 351: Plate, 8½"d, walnuts and leaves, gold trim, artist signed, "Vokral." H&CO. Mark 12 in green and a Pickard decorating mark.

PLATE 352

PLATE 353

PLATE 354

PLATE 355

PLATE 352: Plate, 8¾"d, large white flowers with wide gold band inner border, artist signed, "F. Wallace." H&CO. Mark 13 in green and a Pickard decorating mark.

PLATE 353: Plate, 8½"d, clusters of pink flowers on inner border and in center, gold outer border, artist signed, "John." C.J. Ahrenfeldt Mark 4 in green and a Pickard decorating mark.

PLATE 354: Celery Dish, 12"l, 7¾"w, red berries with small pink flowers decorate center, gold trim, artist signed, "E. Challinor." T&V Mark 7 in green and a Pickard decorating mark.

PLATE 355: Cake Plate, 10½"d, scenic decoration of castle and river with trees in foreground, gold trim, artist signed, "Yeschek." B&Co. Mark 2 in green and a Pickard decorating mark.

PLATE 356: Portrait Plate, 8¼"d, pierced edge, late Victorian lady's portrait made from a transfer of a photograph. GDM Mark 2 in green.

PLATE 357: Souvenir Plate, 8½"d, center is decorated with a transfer of the Court House in Bloomington, Illinois, rose garland around inner border, gold outer border. T&V Mark 8 in green and "Parritt Jewelry Co., Bloomington, Ill. Keramic Photo Process Made in America by Chicago China Decorating Works, Chicago."

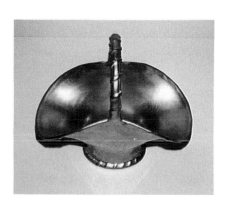

PLATE 358

PLATE 358: Basket, 6"x6", overall gold finish. B&CO. Mark 2 in green and a Stouffer decorating studio mark.

PLATE 359

PLATE 360

PLATE 361

PLATE 362

PLATE 359: Creamer and Open Sugar Bowl, Art Deco shaped handles, orchid flowers and black elliptical designs outlined in gold, artist signed, "R.H." (Robert Hessler). T&V Mark 7 in green and a Pickard decorating mark.

PLATE 360: Tea Set: Creamer, Tea Pot, Open Sugar, heavy silver overlay in an Art Nouveau design by an unknown American silver company. B&CO. Mark 1 in green.

PLATE 361: Cup and Saucer, wide border design of red and green flowers and gold stencilled work. C.J. Ahrenfeldt Mark 4 in green and "A-B Boston" in a red block as decorating mark.

PLATE 362: Bouillon Cup and Saucer, pedestal base, monogrammed "G" in gold with handles and trim painted gold by a professional American decorator. C.J. Ahrenfeldt Mark 4 in green.

American Quality Decoration

PLATE 363: Vase, 14"h, 3 ornately shaped feet, pink, white, and red roses on green background, gold trim on neck. Guérin Mark 3 in green.

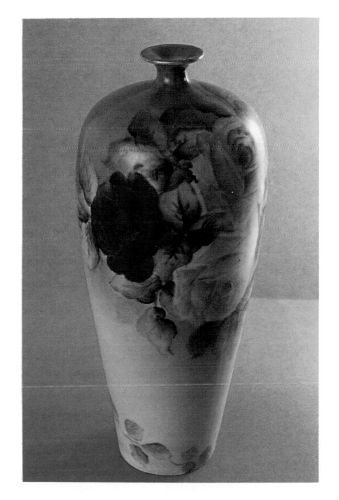

PLATE 364: Vase, 14"h, small neck, large red and pink roses, green leaves on pale green to darker green background. T&V Mark 7 in green.

PLATE 365

PLATE 367

PLATE 366

PLATE 368

PLATE 365: Vase, 9"h, canteen shape, applied branch and flower handles and feet; winter scenic decor, gold brush work on neck with handles and feet heavily gilded. Redon Mark 2 in green.

PLATE 366: Cider Pitcher, 6½"h, red grapes and green leaves on shaded rust colored background, wide gold border. Guérin Mark 3 in green.

PLATE 367: Humidor, 6½"h, vivid red-orange flowers on matte cream finish, sponged gold work, heavy gold trim. T&V Mark 1 in green.

PLATE 368: Jardiniere, large size, ornately scalloped feet and handles painted gold; multi-colored flowers. D&CO. Mark 3 in green.

PLATE 369

PLATE 370

PLATE 371

PLATE 372

PLATE 369: Vase or Loving Cup, 7"h, 3 handles ornately scrolled and heavily gilded, pink and red roses, artist initialed on base, "M.E.J." T&V Mark 8 in green.

PLATE 370: Jardiniere, 6½"h, 6"d, yellow chrysanthemums, gold border. B&CO. Mark 1 in green.

PLATE 371: Cachepot, 9"h, 7½"w, ball feet and ring shaped handles decorated in gold, pink and red roses on pale green background. Guérin Mark 3 in green.

PLATE 372: Vase, 16"h, 10"w, blue and green parrots on floral branches, highly glazed black background. B&CO. Mark 1 in green.

141

PLATE 373

PLATE 374

PLATE 375

PLATE 373: Picture Frame, 9"h, 6½"w, deeply scalloped border, embossed designs outlined in gold, small violet flowers. T&V Mark 5a in green.

PLATE 374: Vase, 13"h, purple irises on matte cream background, scalloped foot and neck brushed with gold, enamelled work on neck. Guérin Mark 2 in green.

PLATE 375: Whiskey Jug, 7"h, multi-colored roses, gold trim. T&V Mark 7 in green.

PLATE 376

PLATE 377

PLATE 378

PLATE 379

PLATE 376: Mug, 5½"h, red cherries, gold trim on neck, Vignaud Mark 1 in green.

PLATE 377: Mug, 5¾"h, blackberries and white blossoms. Guérin Mark 3 in green.

PLATE 378: Mug, 5¾"h, blackberries and pink and white blossoms. T&V Mark 7 in green.

PLATE 379: Tankard, 14½"h, Monk in wine cellar painted in brown tones. Guérin Mark 3 in green.

PLATE 380: Mug, 6"h, figural portrait of a portly gentleman smoking a pipe and holding a glass of wine, artist signed, "Whitridge." Pouyat Mark 5 in green.

PLATE 381: Punch Bowl, 9"h, 14"d, separate footed base; white and purple grapes, heavy gold trim. T&V Mark 7 in green.

PLATE 382

PLATE 384

PLATE 383

PLATE 385

PLATE 382: Charger, 13"d, large pink flowers with green leaves on shaded white to green background, gold trim. Pouyat Mark 5 in green.

PLATE 383: Charger, 12½"d, large pink flowers with green leaves decorate left half of plate. A. Klingenberg Mark 6 in green.

PLATE 384: Tray, 18½"d, irregular border trimmed in gold, red and yellow roses with green leaves on shaded gray to green background. T&V Mark 7 in green.

PLATE 385: Charger, 17"d, pink and yellow roses on dark pink shading to white background, gold trim. T&V Mark 7 in green.

PLATE 386a

PLATE 386b

PLATE 387

PLATE 389

PLATE 388

PLATE 386a: Powder Box, 4½"d, cherubs on pale blue background. T&V Mark 5a in green.

PLATE 386b: Powder Jar, 4"d, lid monogrammed in gold with gold trim. GDM Mark 2 in green.

PLATE 387: Plate, 8½"d, white flowers, pale green leaves, gold trim. T&V Mark 8 in green.

PLATE 388: Cake Plate, 10"d, swags and geometric designs in gold around inner border, gold medallion in center, gold trim. GDA Mark 1 in green.

PLATE 389: Plate, 8½"d, deeply scalloped border forming a wavy design; large leaves tinted light green and pink, outlined in gold, artist signed (illegible). Pouyat Mark 3 in green.

PLATE 390

PLATE 391

PLATE 392

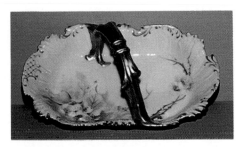

PLATE 393

PLATE 394

PLATE 395

PLATE 390: Pitcher, 6"h, large lip, violets on deep cream background, gold trim. GDM Mark 1 in green.

PLATE 391: Mustard Pot with Underplate, large orange and yellow flowers, brushed gold work, artist initials on base. H&CO. Mark 9 in green.

PLATE 392: Basket, 7"l, small orange flowers with green leaves on shaded brown background; leaf design and beaded shapes on handle decorated in gold. T&V Mark 8 in green.

PLATE 393: Basket, 7½"l, ribbon and bow shaped handle painted gold, pink and white flowers on interior, gold trim. T&V Mark 5a in green.

PLATE 394: Biscuit Jar, 6"h, pink and yellow enamelled floral garlands, gold trim. GDM Mark 2 in green.

PLATE 395: Basket, 4"l, gold outlining on embossed designs on handle and body, tinted pink finish. T&V Mark 5a in green.

PLATE 396

PLATE 397

PLATE 398

PLATE 399

PLATE 400

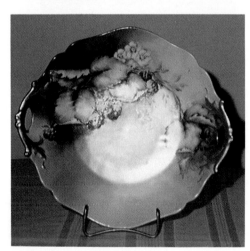

PLATE 401

PLATE 396: Mayonnaise Dish and attached Underplate, 6"x 3", leaf shape with fluted borders, heavily gilded with Art Nouveau style floral design in gold. T&V Mark 7 in green.

PLATE 397: Nappy, 6"x6", white and red roses, gold trim, artist signed (illegible). Pouyat Mark 5 in green.

PLATE 398: Bowl, 12"l, 9"w, free form shape, green leaves around inner border, gold trim. H&C Mark in green.

PLATE 399: Cake plate, 11½"d, small peach roses and white blossoms connected with light green vines, gold trim. Pouyat Mark 5 in green (with Nov. 1882 patent date).

PLATE 400: Charger, 14"d, small purple flowers, green leaves, gold trim. Guérin Mark 2 in green.

PLATE 401: Cake Plate, 10½"d, blackberries on shaded green background, gold handles. D&CO. Mark 3 in green.

PLATE 402

PLATE 403

PLATE 404

PLATE 405

PLATE 402: Occupational Shaving Mug, "Bricklayer," 4"h, 3"d. T&V Mark 7 in green.

PLATE 403: Inkwell, 3"h, 2"sq with Pen Tray, 7"l, floral reserves with pattern of brown scrolled designs on lighter brown background. Limoges, France Mark 6 in green.

PLATE 404: Tobacco Jar, 6"h, applied pipe on lid painted gold; large orange poppies on rust-orange background. T&V Mark 7 in green.

PLATE 405: Shaving Mug, 3½"h, "P. H. Reegan," inscribed in gold, gold trim. H&CO. Mark 8 in green.

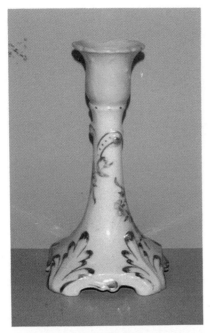

PLATE 406

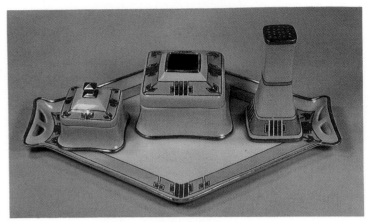

PLATE 408

PLATE 407

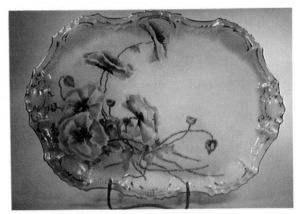

PLATE 409

PLATE 406: Candle Holder, 6"h, scalloped base with leaf forms outlined in gold on white body; cream finish on neck. Pouyat Mark 5 in green.

PLATE 407: Hand Mirror, 9"l, 5"d, lavender and white flowers. T&V Mark 5a in green.

PLATE 408: Dresser Set: Tray, 13"l, Hair Receiver, 4"sq, Pin Box, 2¾" sq., Talcum Shaker, 4"h; blue and gold abstract designs in an Art Deco style, gold trim. Talcum Shaker has La Porcelaine Limousine Mark 2 in green, and the other pieces have Limoges, France Mark 6 in green.

PLATE 409: Dresser Tray, 14"l, crimped and scalloped border, large peach colored flowers and green leaves, gold trim on border and embossed designs. Coiffe Mark 3 in green.

American Amateur Decoration

PLATE 410: 12½"h, 12"w, heavily scrolled base and handles, red and white roses on front with orange and yellow roses on back (not shown), artist initialed on bottom "C.E.M., June, 1892." Pouyat Mark 5 in green.

PLATE 411

PLATE 412

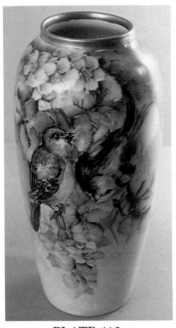

PLATE 413

PLATE 414

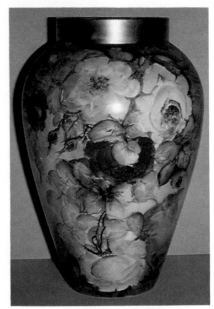

PLATE 415

PLATE 411: Vase, 7"h, 8"d, bulbous body with wide neck, large multi-colored flowers, embossed designs on gilded neck. Pouyat Mark 5 in green.

PLATE 412: Vase, 12", large red and yellow roses, artist signed "Shaver" on face and "A. Niel Brown" on bottom. T&V mark 7 in green.

PLATE 413: Vase, 9 ½"h, pair of bluebirds perched among pink flowers, gold trim. B&CO. Mark 1 in green.

PLATE 414: Vase, 8"h, ovoid shape, red roses, gold trim on neck. D&CO. Mark 3 in green.

PLATE 415: Vase, 14"h, 9"w, multi-colored roses, wide gold border, B&CO. Mark 1 in green.

PLATE 416: Vase, 12"h, 7"w, large pink and white roses on shaded background. B&CO. Mark 1 in green.

PLATE 416

152

PLATE 417

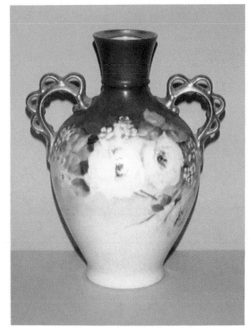

PLATE 418

PLATE 419

PLATE 420

PLATE 417: Vase, 9"h, large curved handles shaped to touch neck, white daisies, brown finish on upper half of vase and handles, artist signed. Pouyat Mark 5 in green.

PLATE 418: Vase, 7"h, fancy scalloped and pierced handles, large white roses on pale green background shading to dark green, artist signed and dated "1898." D&CO. Mark 2 in green.

PLATE 419: Vase, 9"h, rounded body with applied handles, light pink roses on shaded blue-green background, gold trim. Pouyat Mark 5 in green.

PLATE 420: Vase, 4"h, 7"w, small flared neck, red poppies, gold trim. Pouyat Mark 5 in green.

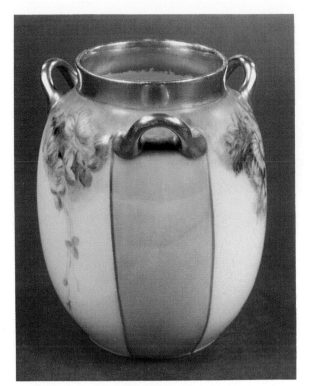

PLATE 421

PLATE 423

PLATE 424

PLATE 422

PLATE 421: Vase, 5½"h, three handles, violet flowers on light to dark blue background. H&CO. Mark 12 in green.

PLATE 422: Vase, 7"h, round body with short neck, pink flowers on pale green background. D&CO. Mark 3 in green.

PLATE 423: Vase, 16"h, cylinder shaped, multi-colored roses on pale green background. Guérin Mark 3 in green

PLATE 424: Vase, 18"h, 8"w, Art Deco style shape, large white roses on light green background, gold trim. Pouyat Mark 5 in green.

PLATE 425

PLATE 426

PLATE 427

PLATE 428

PLATE 425: 8"h, Gibson Girl style portrait framed with gold scrolled work, heavily gilded handles and feet. Redon Mark 2 in green.

PLATE 426: Vase, 11½"h, figural portraits of white robed women and cherub. La Porcelaine Limousine Mark 1 in green.

PLATE 427: Tankard, 14⅝"h, figural portrait of a Monk drinking wine, painted in brown tones with embossed designs on body outlined in gold combined with gold scroll work. T&V Mark 7 in green.

PLATE 428: Whiskey Jug, 6½"h, portrait of a Monk drinking from a wine bottle, dark brown glaze, stopper monogrammed in gold, artist signed on bottom with the year "1905." D&CO. Mark 3 in green.

155

PLATE 429

PLATE 432

PLATE 430

PLATE 433

PLATE 431

PLATE 434

PLATE 429: Ferner, 6"h, 7"d, footed, large orange flowers, green border. D&CO. Mark 3 in green.

PLATE 430: Jardiniere, 8"h, 11"d, purple grapes painted in Art Nouveau style on matte green background. Guérin Mark 3 in green.

PLATE 431: Jardiniere, 6"h, 8"w, purple flowers on matte cream background, gold stars and dots around border. D&CO. Mark 3 in green.

PLATE 432: Jardiniere, 9"h, 11"d, large pink roses on light green body, artist signed, "Mel." B&CO. Mark 1 in green.

PLATE 433: Jardiniere, 7½"h, 11"d, footed with swan neck handles, large pink flowers and green leaves outlined in gold, pearlized interior, heavy gold trim. Paroutaud Mark 2 in green.

PLATE 434: Jardiniere, 12"h, 12"d on separate claw-footed stand, large yellow and red roses on green background, artist signed and dated "1905" on bottom. D&CO. Mark 3 in green.

PLATE 435

PLATE 436

PLATE 437

PLATE 438

PLATE 439

PLATE 440

PLATE 435: Punch Bowl, 14"h, 17"d, footed, purple grapes decorate interior, gold trim. T&V Mark 7 in green.

PLATE 436: Punch Cups, 2½"h, set of 10, red or purple grapes on each cup, matches punch bowl in preceding picture. T&V Mark 8 in green.

PLATE 437: Punch Bowl, 14"d, separate heavily scrolled base, blue grapes and white blossoms. T&V Mark 5a in green.

PLATE 438: Mug, 5¾"h, dragon shaped handle painted gold; red grapes painted in an Art Nouveau style on a pearl lustre background. Pouyat Mark 5 in green.

PLATE 439: Punch Bowl, 6½"h, 14½"d, blackberries and pink blossoms on shaded pink background. T&V Mark 7 in green.

PLATE 440: Punch Bowl, 7"h, 14"d, multi-colored grapes decorate interior and exterior, gold trim, signed "E. Hancock, Nov. 1911." Guérin Mark 3 in green.

157

PLATE 441

PLATE 442

PLATE 443

PLATE 444

PLATE 441: Punch Bowl, 9"h, 13"d, separate heavily scrolled base, on Tray, 16"d with 4 matching mugs; apples decorate exteriors with white blossoms on interior of bowl, black and brown finish on borders, gold trim. T&V Mark 7 in green.

PLATE 442: Punch Bowl, 12¼"h, 8"d, separate claw footed base, purple grapes, gold trim. Pouyat Mark 5 in green.

PLATE 443: Chalice, 10½"h, white and purple grapes framed with gold scroll designs, gold medallions at top and on base, dark wine border, gold trim. Pouyat Mark 5 in green.

PLATE 444: Chalice, 10"h, strawberries decorate bowl stem and base finished in a dark brown glaze, heavy gold trim, artist signed, "T. Sampolis." T&V Mark 7 in green.

158

PLATE 445

PLATE 446

PLATE 447

PLATE 448

PLATE 449

PLATE 450

PLATE 445: Tankard, 13"h, purple grapes and green leaves on shaded green background, dark green base. Pouyat Mark 5 in green.

PLATE 446: Tankard, 14"h, red and black berries with light green leaves on shaded green background, dull gold finish on handle. Guérin Mark 3 in green.

PLATE 447: Tankard, 10½"h, blackberries, dark brown finish on base and sides of handle with gold band painted around middle of base and outer part of handle. T&V Mark 7 in green.

PLATE 448: Tankard, 13½"h, pink and purple grapes, gold handle. Pouyat Mark 5 in green.

PLATE 449: Tankard, 12"h, green and purple grapes, top border and handle painted gold, artist initialed "EPN '09." Pouyat Mark 5 in green.

PLATE 450: Tankard, 12"h, purple and pink grapes on shaded orange background, artist signed, "L.M. Gleason." Pouyat Mark 5 in green.

PLATE 451

PLATE 452

PLATE 453

PLATE 454

PLATE 451: Pitcher, 8½"h, Art Nouveau shape, white berries, light brown leaves, dark green finish on upper border, handle, and base. T&V Mark 6 in green.

PLATE 452: Tankard, 15½"h, applied leaf and curling vine decorate handle in an Art Nouveau style; purple grapes on light green to blue background, artist signed "F. Paxton 1905" on bottom. T&V Mark 7 in green.

PLATE 453: Tankard, 14¾"h, purple grapes, gold handle, undecorated base. Guérin Mark 3 in green.

PLATE 454: Tankard, 12"h, purple and white grapes, gold trim, signed "Au 1902" on face. T&V Mark 7 in green.

160

PLATE 455

PLATE 456

PLATE 457

PLATE 458

PLATE 455: Cake Plate, 10½"d, portrait of Victorian woman with beauty mark, artist signed, "TR Sravry 1898" on bottom. Limoges, France Mark 7 in green.

PLATE 456: Portrait Plaque, 7½"l, lady in Victorian dress with large plumed hat. GDM Mark 2 in green.

PLATE 457: Humidor, 7"h, dark brown finish on bottom half, yellow roses form borders around middle of jar and lid, monogrammed. H&CO. Mark 12 in green.

PLATE 458: Humidor, 7½"h, pink roses and white blossoms on pale green background, gold finial. T&V Mark 7 in green.

PLATE 459

PLATE 460

PLATE 461

PLATE 462

PLATE 463

PLATE 464

PLATE 459: Candle Holders, 7"h, small pink flowers on base, top decorated in gold. Plainemaison Mark in green.

PLATE 460: Cologne Bottle, 5½"h, pink and white roses on shaded blue background, gold trim. Guérin Mark 3 in green.

PLATE 461: Toothbrush Holder, 4"h, a wide border decorated with white blossoms around top of holder, blue background, lid painted gold. Coiffe Mark 3 in green.

PLATE 462: Dresser Box, 5"l, heart shaped, large white flowers with purple shadows. D&CO. Mark 3 in green.

PLATE 463: Dresser Set: Cologne Bottles and Trinket Box; scalloped pedestal feet, red or blue flowers on each piece, gold trim. H&CO. Mark 11 in green.

PLATE 464: Dresser Set: Tray, Powder Box, Hair Receiver, Pin Box, Ring Tray; wide pink border outlined in gold with dark pink roses in clusters around inner border, gold trim. GDA Mark 1 in green.

PLATE 465

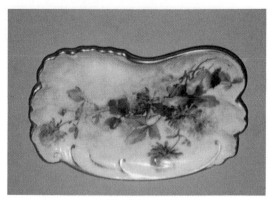

PLATE 466

PLATE 467

PLATE 468

PLATE 469

PLATE 470

PLATE 465: Pin Tray, 6", heart shaped, cluster of pink roses. T&V Mark 7 in green.

PLATE 466: Pin Tray, 5"l, pink and white flowers, gold trim. T&V Mark 7 in green.

PLATE 467: Bonbon Dish, scalloped border brushed with gold, floral pattern in center outlined with gold, artist signed, "MW 1890." GDM Mark 1 in green.

PLATE 468: Basket, 6"x6", pink flowers, gold trim. B&CO. Mark 2 in green.

PLATE 469: Paper Weight, 5½"l, 3"w, quill shape in relief divides the piece, white flowers, gold trim. T&V Mark 5a in green.

PLATE 470: Stamp Box, 4"l, blue flowers on lid, gold trim originally outlined the embossed scroll designs on body. H&CO. Mark 11 in green.

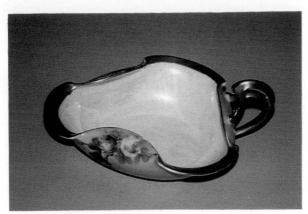

Plate 471

Plate 472

Plate 473

Plate 474

Plate 475

Plate 476

PLATE 471: Nappy, 7"x 5½", pink roses on green background, gold trim, pearlized luster finish on interior. T&V Mark 7 in green.

PLATE 472: Leaf Dishes, 4½"x 3", one decorated with flowers and the other with nuts on shaded brown background. T&V Mark 7 in green.

PLATE 473: Leaf Dish, 6"x5", large white daisies on shaded blue background, gold trim. Guérin Mark 3 in green.

PLATE 474: Trinket Box, 3½"h, 10"d, large roses, gold and turquoise enamelling painted on center of lid, outer border of lid and base painted black, signed "Adolph Anderson, 1899" on bottom. Bawo & Dotter Mark 5 in green.

PLATE 475: Bowl, 12"l, footed with large curved handles, red berries on green background on exterior with berries and leaves painted in sepia tones on interior. H&CO. Mark 11 in green.

PLATE 476: Tray, 11"l, 6"w, split center handle painted gold, red and white flowers, artist signed on bottom. Guérin Mark 3 in green.

PLATE 477

PLATE 481

PLATE 478

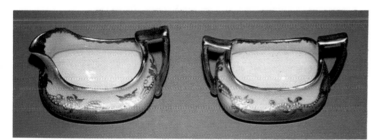

PLATE 479

PLATE 482

PLATE 480

PLATE 477: Sugar Basket, 5"d, and Creamer, pink and yellow flowers on light green background, gold trim. Pouyat Mark 5 in green.

PLATE 478: Mug, 5"h, multi-colored grapes, artist signed "E. Kluchharm." Pouyat Mark 5 in green.

PLATE 479: Creamer and Open Sugar Bowl, 3½"h, gold beaded designs on light blue background. T&V Mark 7 in green.

PLATE 480: Pitcher, 3½"h, large white water lilies. Paroutaud Mark 2 in green.

PLATE 481: Child's Mug, 2½"h, pink and white flowers. H&CO. Mark 11 in green.

PLATE 482: Child's Cup and Saucer, pink and white flowers, gold trim. GDM Mark 2 in green.

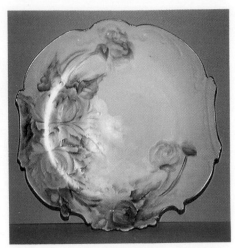

PLATE 483

PLATE 486

PLATE 484

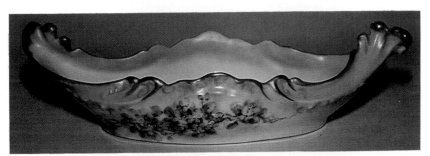

PLATE 487

PLATE 485

PLATE 488

PLATE 483: Bowl, 11"d, deeply scalloped border forms handles; pink, yellow, and purple flowers, gold trim. Guérin Mark 3 in green.

PLATE 484: Covered Vegetable Bowl, 12"l, shaded light blue finish, gold band borders, gold trim on handles and finials. Charles Field Haviland Mark 1 in green.

PLATE 485: Bowl, 9"d, scalloped shells form border, deep pink glaze, gold trim. Lanternier Mark 3 in green.

PLATE 486: Plate, 8½"d, irregular shape in an Art Nouveau style; small flowers shading from white to orange, pale blue border decorated with gold scroll work and criss-cross designs. Bawo & Dotter Mark 4 in green.

PLATE 487: Relish Dish, 10"l, 4"w, fancy scalloped design forms handles on each end; small pink and blue flowers on shaded blue background, gold trim. Pouyat Mark 5 in green.

PLATE 488: Cake Plate, 11½"d, predominantly pink roses on shaded blue background with handles painted gold. T&V Mark 7 in green.

PLATE 489

PLATE 490

PLATE 491

PLATE 492

PLATE 493

PLATE 494

PLATE 489: Plate, 9"d, reticulated border painted gold; chain of white flowers around center. T&V Mark 6 in green.

PLATE 490: Plate, 9"d, same reticulated mold as one in preceding picture; cherub decorates center, light green background. T&V Mark 5a in green.

PLATE 491: Charger, 12½"d, scalloped and beaded border painted gold with gold designs and pink roses forming pattern around inner border, light green background. T&V Mark 5a in green.

PLATE 492: Tray, 13½"d, pine cones with green pine needles, shaded brown background. T&V Mark 7 in green.

PLATE 493: Plaque, 17"d, framed, purple and white grapes on pale green background. T&V Mark 7 in green.

PLATE 494: Finger Bowl, 3½"d with Underplate, 5½"d; pale pink flowers on interior with exterior of bowl and underplate decorated in green with gold trim. GDA Mark 1 in green.

PLATE 495

PLATE 496

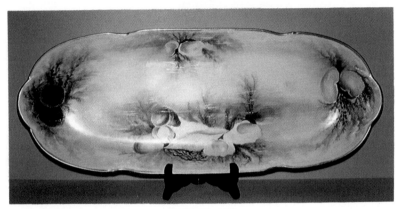

PLATE 497

PLATE 498

PLATE 499

PLATE 500

PLATE 495: Plates, 8½"d, set of 6 from Fish Set; beaded border decorated in gold, underwater scene of shells and seaweed. See matching decoration in the following two photographs. Note that the blanks are different. Pouyat Mark 5 in green.

PLATE 496: Seafood Serving Dish, 11"l, 6"w, divided (large side for seafood and smaller side for sauce), decorated with mollusks similar to preceding plates. T&V Mark 8 in green.

PLATE 497: Fish Platter, 24"l, 10"w, decoration matches preceding plates and serving dish. D&CO. Mark 3 in green.

PLATE 498: Ice Cream Serving Tray, 16½"l, 8½"d, pink flowers, gold trim, artist signed and dated "1913." Paroutaud Mark 1 in green.

PLATE 499: Celery Tray, 13"l, 6"w, orange poppies on shaded green background. Gold trim. A. Klingenberg Mark 7 in green.

PLATE 500: Bowl, 14"l, 9½"d, heavily scalloped border with large scallop forming handle; butterflies and multi-colored flowers decorate center, brushed gold work on border. GDM Mark 1 in green.

ALPHABETICAL LISTING OF LIMOGES FACTORIES AND STUDIOS

Limoges factories, decorating studios, and unidentified companies and decorators are listed here in alphabetical order with brief comments and histories according to information available for each. The marks used by these companies follow this listing, also arranged alphabetically and numbered only within companies. Consult the Index And Cross Reference To Companies, Initials, and Symbols if a particular mark, symbol, or name is not found.

A&D

These initials are found as an overglaze decorating mark in either red or green. The decorating studio is unidentified. From examples, the mark appears to have been in use during the late 1800's.

AHRENFELDT, CHARLES (CA)

Charles Ahrenfeldt was born in Germany in 1807. He was connected with several different aspects of the porcelain business during his life. He was engaged in the china importing business in New York in the 1830's. During the 1840s, he moved to Paris where he had a studio for decorating porcelain. He is noted to have been located in Limoges from about 1860. There he first had an export firm and later a decorating studio circa 1884. It is probable that before his death, in 1893, he had started the Ahrenfeldt factory for manufacturing porcelain which was continued by his son. One mark is shown in the Marks section which is attributed to Charles Ahrenfeldt's decorating studio in Limoges. (See Ahrenfeldt, Charles J.)

AHRENFELDT, CHARLES J. (CA)

Charles J. Ahrenfeldt was born in 1856. He carried on the porcelain business established by his father, Charles Ahrenfeldt, and began producing porcelain about 1894. During the late 1890s, the company carried on an extensive export trade. White wares and decorated table china were the principal articles manufactured. Factory decorated pieces are double marked with the white ware mark in green underglaze and the decorating mark in various colors overglaze. The dates when the various marks were used is not totally clear and reference sources cite conflicting dates for some of the marks. The firm had a long history, active except during the war years, until about 1969. A number of white ware marks were used as well as several different decorating marks. Mark 1 is probably the earliest mark used by Charles J. It is overglaze in blue and is found as a decorating mark on porcelain manufactured by other Limoges companies. It is the same mark as that used by his father, except for the color and the addition of the words "Limoges, France." It is not the elder Ahrenfeldt's mark because some examples have the white ware mark of factories established after the senior Ahrenfeldt's death. The mark is after 1893 and was probably used before the factory was producing and decorating to full capacity. The white ware marks (see Marks 2-6) were probably used at different periods, but all of these, with the exception of Mark 3 (no example seen) have either been alone or with Mark 8, an overglaze decorating mark in green or gold. Mark 4 has also been seen with decorating Mark 7 in green. Marks 2 through 8 were probably used until World War II. Mark 9 which incorporates the white ware mark in its design appears to be a mid twentieth century mark.

AJCO

These initials appear as a fancy monogram in an overglaze decorating mark in blue. The decorating studio is unidentified. The example and type of mark indicate that this studio operated during the 1930s or later.

ALLUAUD, FRANÇOIS

François Alluaud became director of the Royal Limoges Porcelain Company in 1788. He served in this capacity until 1794 when the operations were disrupted by the French Revolution. The company was sold to three workers, one of whom, Joly, leased his share to Alluaud. Thus in control of a section of the kaolin deposits, Alluaud sold paste to other companies. This paste was of an exceptional quality and is credited for the fame which Limoges porcelain acquired. Alluaud established his own porcelain factory about 1798, but he died shortly thereafter in 1799. (See Alluaud, François, II.)

ALLUAUD, FRANÇOIS, II (AF)

After the death of his father, François Alluaud, II took over the operation of the Alluaud factory. The Alluaud company became the largest in Limoges during the first half of the nineteenth century. A variety of decorative objects were manufactured. Additionally, the company sold its white wares to other companies and decorators. A large export business was conducted with other European countries and the United States. The business remained directly in the Alluaud family until around 1876 when it was taken over by Charles Field Haviland. Marked examples of the Alluaud company are rarely found in this country although a few marks were used and are shown in the Marks section. (See Haviland, Charles Field.)

ALUMINITE (FRG)

René Frugier owned this Limoges factory. "Aluminite" refers to the special porcelain cook ware the company manufactured. The factory was established about 1900. It survived both World Wars, but it was eventually taken over by the Haviland Company about 1964 (d'Albis and Romanet, p. 152). A variety of marks was used by the company, but dating is inexact. Most of the marks were used during the 1920s. Few examples are found in this country.

ARDANT, HENRI

Henri Ardant was in business in Limoges from about 1859 until the early 1880s. The company was noted for its artistic production which appears not to have been geared to export to the United States. A distinctive "bird on a branch" mark was used by this company.

A V

These initials were used by an unidentified factory as an impressed mark. Examples with this mark were decorated with the popular Moss Rose design, but the pieces did not have a decorating mark. The impressed mark might possibly be that of Aragon and Vultury who operated in Limoges during the 1880s, a time when such decoration was common.

BALLEROY, H. (B&Cie.)

Henri Balleroy was associated with Mandavy and Mavaleix from about 1901 until 1908. In 1908, Henri and his brother, Antoine, formed a company. They manufactured decorative accessories and table wares. In the first edition, two decorating marks were attributed to this firm. Later research indicates that these are marks of other factories (see B. H. and B. & H.). The only decorating mark noted for this company is a printed mark "Porcelaines, HA Balleroy Frères, Limoges." The company closed in the late 1930s.

BARNY and RIGONI

Barny and Rigoni established a porcelain factory about 1894. In 1902, J. Redon, son of Martial Redon, joined the firm. At that time the marks of the factory changed to include the Redon name. Note that the initial "M" rather than "J" was used to capitalize on the earlier M. Redon company. This set of partners continued until about 1904 when Redon left and Langle became an associate. This partnership lasted only a few years before other owners took charge, changing the name to La Porcelaine Limousine. Very few examples with any of the marks associated with the firm are seen. (See La Porcelaine Limousine.)

BASSETT

Table china decorated in floral patterns are found with the Bassett mark. The company was an American based importing firm. Factories in Limoges and Austria produced table wares designed for the American market and stamped them with the Bassett mark in red or green. Pieces do not have a white ware mark but were decorated at the factory which produced them. From examples, the time period for this company would be the late 1800s until World War I, coinciding with the time when several American businesses were engaged in the porcelain importing trade in both Limoges and Austria.

BAWO & DOTTER (ELITE WORKS)

Bawo & Dotter was established in the 1860s in New York City for the purpose of importing china, notably Limoges porcelain, for the American consumer. The firm set up its own decorating studio in Limoges during the early 1870s which was named The Elite Works. The company did not begin manufacturing its own china until about 1896 (d'Albis and Romanent, p. 126). From the 1870s through the 1890s, the company decorated the white ware made by other Limoges factories. Many example of Bawo & Dotter's decoration and porcelain are found in a variety of decorative items and table wares.

The earliest marks used by the company appear to be Marks 1–3, a bottle shape incorporating the Arms of Limoges. While exact dating is not possible, it is reasonable to assign certain periods to the marks based on examples bearing such marks and by comparing the white ware marks of other companies found in conjunction with the Bawo & Dotter decorating marks. Later decorating marks are very similar and also include the Arms of Limoges. The white ware marks seem to show the transition from only decorating to manufacturing with the underglaze mark being similar to the decorating mark (see Marks 4 and 8). Each mark has "Limoges" written in script form.

The company's production was interrupted in Limoges during World War I. After the War, circa 1920, the company purchased the William Guérin firm, and the name of the company became Guérin-Pouyat-Elite, Ltd. (Guérin had previously purchased the Pouyat company.) The individual marks of each of the three companies appear to have been continued from the time of this merger until the business closed in 1932. Apparently, undecorated blanks by either of the three companies were used with a new mark of Guerin-Pouyat-Elite, Ltd. (see Bawo & Dotter Mark 12). This mark is rarely seen, and information on exactly when it was put in use after 1920 has not been found.

BEAUX-ARTS

Beaux-Arts is an unidentified decorating studio. The mark was found on an example decorated in an Art Nouveau floral style, placing the mark circa 1900.

BERNARDAUD, LEON (B& CO.)

Leon Bernardaud was the successor to the Délinères (D&CO.) factory. He and his father had worked for the earlier company. There appears to be some misunderstanding concerning the time when the company actually became known as Bernardaud and Company. The year 1863 is often cited for the date of its founding. However, this date actually marks the beginning of the Guéry firm which preceded Guéry and Délinières. The Bernardaud Company succeeded Délinières & Co. about 1900 (d'Albis and Romanet, p. 160). The early white ware marks (Mark 1) of Bernardaud closely resemble the style of Délinières' Marks, and examples are found with the D&CO. white ware mark and the decorating mark of Bernardaud, indicating a transition in ownership. Leon Bernardaud's company was continued by his family and is currently in operation. Examples of the factory's production from the early 1900s through the 1920s are primarily in the form of white wares which have handpainted decoration by American china painters. The decorating Mark is usually found on dinner ware with transfer decor. Note that while Mark 2 is sometimes noted as being in use after 1930, the mark was probably in use after World War I. One example shown with Mark 2 also has a decorating mark used by the American Pickard decorating studio which was in use from 1912–1919 (Platt, p. 74). This decorating mark, of course, had to have been applied after the white ware mark used by Bernardaud. (See Délinières, R.)

B. H.

These initials printed inside a small shield appear as an underglaze white ware mark in green. In the first edition, this mark was attributed to H. Balleroy, but later research seems to indicate that this is the mark of another company. Very few pieces have been seen with this mark. From examples, the mark was used during the 1920s.

B. & H.

These initials, printed in a double circle with "Limoges, France," are found as an overglaze decorating mark on decorative pieces and table wares. The studio using this mark remains unidentified. The mark could possibly have been used by Blakeman and Henderson. Examples have various white ware marks, including those of Coiffe and Plainemaison, which help to place the time period for the mark in the late 1890s.

BLAKEMAN & HENDERSON

Blakeman & Henderson appears to have been only a decorating studio. Their full name mark is an overglaze mark in green, written in script form. The Coiffe mark or other Limoges factories' white ware marks are seen with this decorating mark. Examples indicate that the mark was used during the late 1890s. Another decorating mark with these initials (B. & H.) is also found on decorative pieces and table wares. It is possible that this is also a Blakeman & Henderson mark, perhaps predating the fancier script mark. Until this is authenticated, however, the B&H mark will be listed separately. (See B&H.)

BOISBERTRAND

The Boisbertrand Company was in business from about 1884 until the late 1930s. Boisbertrand was associated with several different people during those years. The only mark noted for this company is an ambiguous one with "Limoges" printed inside a banner. This particular mark was used during the 1920s. Lack of examples indicates that the production was not geared to export to the United States.

BORGFELDT, GEORGE (CORONET)

George Borgfeldt operated a New York based importing company with art studios located in France and Germany. The studio was located in Paris but decorated porcelain manufactured by various factories in Limoges. The Coiffe white ware mark is often seen on items with the Borgfeldt "Coronet" mark. Many examples, however, do not have a white ware mark. Expertly and richly decorated plaques and plates with game bird, floral, and figural themes carry the Coronet mark. Artist signed pieces are in great demand. Some dinner ware patterns also have the Borgfeldt mark. Decorated pieces date form the early 1900s, ca. 1906 to the 1920s. Mark 2, with " Trade Mark" is later than Mark 1.

BOYER, JEAN

Jean Boyer established a porcelain factory in Limoges circa 1919. He was succeeded by his son, George, during the mid 1930s. Few examples are found with Boyer's marks.

B.S.

These initials printed in a star are found as an underglaze white ware mark in green. The company is unidentified. The decorating mark of Serpaut was on the example, but the white ware mark cannot be documented as one used by Serpaut. The time period for the mark would be the late 1920s.

C. et J.

These initials are the basis for an overglaze decorating mark in red. The studio is unidentified. The mark was found on a handpainted game bird plate. The matching plate had a "Coronet" mark. The C. et J. mark would date from circa the late 1800s to 1914.

C. H.

These initials with the Seal of Limoges were found as an underglaze white ware mark on a fish set decorated by Bawo & Dotter (Elite Works). The C. H. mark has not been identified. It is interesting to note that the decorating mark used by Bawo & Dotter also has the same Seal or Arms of Limoges. No information has surfaced to indicate if Bawo and Dotter took over a factory which used such a seal as its white ware mark, with Bawo and Dotter subsequently adapting it as a decorating mark. The C. H. mark would date from the 1880s or earlier to 1890. (See Bawo & Dotter.)

CHABROL FRÈRES and POIRER (C.F. & P.)

This Limoges company was in business from about 1917 until the late 1930s. The only mark noted for this company is designed with a pair of wings and a star which was used during the 1920s.

CHAUFFRAISSE, ROUGERIE, & CO. (L. HERMITAGE)

This factory was in business from circa 1925 to the mid 1930s. A distinctive mark incorporating a house with "L. Hermitage" printed above and the initials "C. R." printed below was used by the factory during the late 1920s.

CMC or GMC

A monogram mark with these initials (it is unclear whether the first letter is a "C" or a "G") is an underglaze white ware mark in green. The factory is unidentified. The time period for the mark is circa after 1890 until 1914.

COIFFE

The distinctive star mark used by the Coiffe factory is one of the most frequently seen on various pieces of Limoges porcelain. The factory produced a large amount of blanks which were decorated by other Limoges factories or studios, or by American china painters. The mark is usually accompanied by the decorating mark of another firm. When the Coiffe mark is the only mark on an object, the decoration in some instances appears to be professional, but whether the company actually decorated any china is not known. Some examples are definitely professionally decorated, and some obviously are not. It is evident that the factory manufactured excellent quality porcelain, often ornately fashioned, ranging from table china to decorative accessories. The company had several associates during its history which dates from the 1870s to the mid 1920s. The same mark is shown for L. Coiffe and E. Coiffe Jeune (Junior) by Lesur and Tardy (1967, pp. 55; 108) with L. Coiffe noted as being in business during the mid 1870s, and E. Coiffe Jeune operating in Limoges from 1887.

COMTE D'ARTOIS

An overglaze mark in the form of a decal incorporates this name with a crown. The mark is a late twentieth century one and should not be confused as being a mark used by the first Limoges factory which was under the protection of the Comte d' Artois.

CRÉANGE, HENRI

Henri Créange was shown in the first edition to have used the trade mark "Old Abbey." Lesur and Tardy (1967, p. 111) list Créange as a *negociant*, and illustrate an "Old Abbey" mark used by him in 1907. D'Albis and Romanet (p. 192), however, indicate that Latrille Frères used an "Old Abbey" mark, and that "Old Abbey" actually refers to the factory which had been an Abbey at one time. Examples with the "Old Abbey" mark shown by Lesur and Tardy, however, often have the white ware mark used by Latrille Frères (see Latrille Frères). Another version of an "Old Abbey" mark was found in conjunction with the HC monogram which was attributed to Créange in the first edition. It is possible that all "Old Abbey" marks are related, but until further information is available, the two different types of "Old Abbey" marks will be separated with one shown for Créange and the other shown for Latrille Frères.

DÉLINIÈRES, REMY (D&CO.)

Remy Délinières was associated with P. Guéry during the 1860s. No marks have been attributed to the association of Guéry and Délinières. According to d'Albis and Romanet (pp. 161, 162), Délinières became head of the company after 1879. In 1900, the company became L. Bernardaud and Co. Marks 1 and 2 represent early white ware marks, and Mark 4 is an early decorating mark. These were in use before 1891. Wood (p. 31) notes that the Délinières Company did not decorate its production until after 1881 when they established a decorating workshop at the factory. Mark 4 is the first decorating mark used by the company. It was continued until 1893, according to Wood. Mark 3 is the most commonly seen D&CO mark, dating after 1891 until 1900. It is found on many decorative white wares which have American handpainted decoration. Factory decorated items with Mark 5, an overglaze mark in red of "R. Délinières, Limoges" written in script form, are usually table wares. Some decorative fish and game services can also be found with factory decoration. Pieces which appear to be factory decorated are sometimes found without an overglaze decorating mark. (See Bernardaud, L.)

DEMARTINE, G. (G. D. & CIE.)

The Demartine factory was in business during the late 1800s. Examples show that the company manufactured and decorated china. The marks shown are after 1891 until the early 1900s.

DWENGER, CHARLES (AKCD)

Charles Dwenger operated a New York based importing company. He imported china from both Limoges and Austria. Dwenger appears to have been associated with A. Klingenberg at Limoges because marks incorporate both Klingenberg's and Dwenger's initials and follow the same style. The exact time when Klingenberg and Dwenger became partners, or if Dwenger actually took over the Klingenberg company is not known. The mark showing Dwenger's association with Klingenberg is shown with the Klingenberg marks. (See Klingenberg, A.)

E. G. D. & CO.

These initials with "Couleurs Feu De Four" and "Inalterables" appear as an overglaze decorating mark in green. The studio is unidentified. The mark was on an example of GDM white ware decorated with a flow-blue type floral decor. The mark would have been in use during the 1890s.

FLAMBEAU CHINA (LDB&C)

This company was listed in the first edition as L. D. & C. Subsequent discovery of two other marks, however, indicates that the name of the company was probably "Flambeau China." The owners of the company are still unidentified. In many of the marks, the "B" is not clear and looks like an ampersand. The marks found after the first edition was published show the "B" clearly. A mark similar to Mark 5 is also noted to have been used on Bavarian china. Some of the examples carry a white ware mark (see Mark 1), but many pieces only have one of the decorating marks with or without the white ware mark of another Limoges factory. Also some items have the LDB&C decorating mark and no white ware mark. From the dates of the other factories' white ware marks, it is apparent that Flambeau China was in business from the late 1890s until the first World War. Its first operations were also probably confined to decorating rather than manufacturing, and it may well have been an American based company. Examples with the Flambeau marks are highly decorated and often handpainted. No examples have been found of white wares decorated by American artists. The distinctive "torch" and "flame" marks were obviously the insignia for the company's name.

FLORALE

A wreath with "Florale" printed in script is an overglaze decorating mark in green of an unidentified Limoges studio. The mark was found on a Balleroy blank, and from the shape and decoration, the firm was in business during the 1920s.

FONTANILLE AND MARRAUD

This company was established during the mid 1930s and is still in operation. The company was also known as Porcelaine Artistique. Gift and souvenir objects were products of the company as well as miniatures and artistic wares.

FRANÇOIS, ANDRÉ (AF)

This company was in business from about 1919 until the mid 1930s. Lack of examples indicates that the factory did not export much porcelain to this country.

GÉRARD, DUFRAISSEIX, AND ABBOT (GDA)

These men became partners in 1900 when Abbot joined Gérard and Dufraisseix. Abbot had been connected with the company's import operations in New York City. The back mark of the firm changed at that time to include Abbot's initials. The company also was known as Porcelaines GDA. The company continued to use the Charles Field Haviland decorating mark of the earlier GDM company until about 1941. At that time, the mark (see Mark 3) was sold to the Haviland and Parlon Company (see Haviland, Robert). Note that the

Charles Field Haviland decorating mark used by GDA seems to be always in red, rather than other colors used by its predecessor, GDM.

Objects which have the GDA mark and the Charles Field Haviland mark are later than those with only the CFH mark (see Haviland, Charles Field). After 1941, Mark 4 has been used by GDA. The company is still in operation. The company manufactured white wares, table china, decorative accessories, and art objects. The firm is noted to have made porcelain art objects for the L'Art Nouveau firm of Samuel Bing in Paris during the early 1900s. (See Gérard, Dufraisseix, and Morel.)

GÉRARD, DUFRAISSEIX, AND MOREL (GDM)

This company succeeded the Charles Field Haviland Company about 1882. The CFH initials in the white ware marks were maintained with the addition of the new firm's initials. The same Charles Field decorating mark was used. The company manufactured white wares, table china, decorative accessories, and art objects. Factory decorated pieces are not always double marked with both a white ware and a decorating mark.

Morel ceased to be a partner around 1890, thus leaving the business in the name of Gérard and Dufraisseix until 1900. (See Haviland, Charles Field and Gérard, Dufraisseix, and Abbot.)

GIBUS AND REDON

Gibus and Redon were associated in the porcelain business from the mid 1850s until 1881. The name of the company was Gibus and Cie, however, until 1872 (d'Albis and Romanet, pp. 128, 129). The company manufactured art objects and decorative accessories. Mark 1 is incised, and Mark 2 is a stamped mark in red. Martial Redon took over the company in 1882. Mark 2 is the same type of mark he used as a white ware mark after he took charge of the company. Pieces have been seen with both Marks 1 and 2, but examples obviously factory decorated have been seen with only Mark 1. (See Redon, M.)

GIRAUD, ANDRÉ

André Giraud was in business in Limoges during the 1920s. He became associated with Brousseau during the 1930s. The company produced white wares and decorative accessories. It is still in business today.

GRANGER, J. & CIE

J. Granger became the head of the Mavaleix factory about 1922 after joining the company in 1920. Granger had previously been associated with Latrille Frères from 1908–1913 (d'Albis and Romanet, 1979, p. 92). The white ware mark used by Granger also incorporates Mavaleix's initials. No definite decorating mark has been noted for the company, although "Old Abbey" has sometimes been linked to this firm (see "Old Abbey" Marks under Latrille Frères). Pieces with the Granger marks usually have a decorating mark of another factory or studio or were blanks decorated by American china painters. The business was in operation until about 1938. (See Mavaleix, P. and Latrille Frères.)

GUÉRIN, WILLIAM (WG&CO.)

William Guérin was the successor to the Utzschneider porcelain factory during the early 1870s where Guérin had been director before becoming owner. The firm carried on a large export business. The majority of Guérin pieces available are in the form of table china or white wares decorated in America. In the white ware line, Guérin "cachepots" (literally meaning pots to hide something such as jardinieres or letter holders, depending on size) appear to have been a favorite of American china painters. Factory decorated vases are sometimes found.

Shortly before World War I, the Pouyat firm merged with Guérin. It appears that both Pouyat marks and Guérin marks were used after the merger, but two years after the War, the Guérin Company was purchased by Bawo & Dotter (Elite Works). Due to the war years, from the time Pouyat and Guérin were joined and the short period after the war before the Company was sold, it is difficult to know how much of the new production would have actually carried a Pouyat mark. Probably the remaining Pouyat stock, which was already marked, was sold through the Guérin company, or the former Pouyat factory merely continued producing using the same Pouyat marks prior to the merger.

It is also noted by French references that all three companies' marks were continued after 1920 when Bawo & Dotter purchased the Guérin Company. Bawo & Dotter Mark 12 was found on a Guérin blank, seemingly indicating a new mark showing the merger of all three factories. Examples with this particular mark, however, are rare. Bawo & Dotter closed in 1932, and thus Guérin marks are no later than that year.

Mark 1, WG & Ce (for *compagnie*) is a mark attributed to Guérin when he was associated with Utzschneider. It would date circa the 1870s, and it is rarely found. Mark 2, although incorporating the word "France," should date prior to 1891. Mark 3, with "Limoges" and "France" as part of the mark dates after 1900. This is the mark most frequently found on Guérin examples. Mark 4 is a decorating mark certainly in use after 1891, and perhaps some years earlier. The mark seems to have remained essentially the same with some variation which are infrequently seen and were probably not intended for use on exported wares. Examples of such marks are "Wm. Guérin & Co. de Limoges, France," and "W. Guérin and Cie., Paris & Limoges" printed in an oval shape. A torch with "Guérin Feu de Four" may be found a a mark on some pieces, indicating a special firing process. (See Bawo & Dotter.)

GUTHERZ, OSCAR

Oscar Gutherz and his brother Edgar were involved in the porcelain business in Austria circa 1899. Pieces seen with the Limoge

Gutherz mark do not carry any white ware mark. The Austrian company was especially known for its handpainted decorations, and the work on examples of Limoges Gutherz is very well executed. The company appears to have been only a decorating studio in Limoges during the late 1800s.

HAVILAND AND ABBOT COMPANY

This name reflects the association of Edgar Abbot with the American importing firm of Charles Field Haviland. Abbot did not join this company until about 1886 (d 'Albis and Romanet, p. 148). This occurred after the Limoges factory of Charles Field Haviland became Gérard, Dufraisseix, and Morel. The mark, in fact, is most frequently found in conjunction with GDA white ware marks used after Abbot was named a partner with Gérard and Dufraisseix circa 1900. (See Gérard, Dufraisseix, and Abbot.)

HAVILAND, CHARLES FIELD (CFH)

Charles Field Haviland went to Limoges from America in the early 1850s to work for his uncle, David Haviland (the founder of Haviland and Company). After a few years, however, he left his uncle's firm and established his own porcelain decorating studio. He acquired his first porcelain factory about 1868. Later, he married the granddaughter of François Alluaud, Sr., and in 1876, he took charge of the Alluaud porcelain factory, one of the oldest Limoges companies (see Alluaud). It is possible that early Charles Field decorated items were not marked. Only one form of decorating mark for him has been documented, see Mark 3. This particular mark is most often found on objects made by the successors to his company rather than on pieces carrying only his white ware marks (see Marks 1 and 2). In 1881, Charles Field retired from the business and Gérard, Dufraisseix, and Morel (GDM) took over the operations. The GDM company continued to use Mark 3 but changed the white ware mark to include their initials. Subsequently, the succeeding firm of Gérard, Dufraisseix, and Abbot (circa 1900), continued only Mark 3, using their own initials for the white ware mark. (See Gérard, Dufraisseix, and Morel; Gérard, Dufraisseix, and Abbot; and Robert Haviland.)

HAVILAND, DAVID (H&CO.) and HAVILAND, THEODORE

David Haviland played a very important role in bringing Limoges porcelain to the attention of the American public. He began his career as an importer of French porcelain in New York during the late 1830s and early 1840s. He moved to France in 1841 and settled in Limoges about 1842. Haviland operated an exporting business for several years, choosing porcelain made by Limoges factories to be shipped to his New York company. In 1847, he opened a decorating studio in Limoges. He had other Limoges factories make porcelain items according to his specifications which, in turn, were decorated at his studio and then shipped to New York.

David Haviland did not produce any porcelain until 1865 (d'Albis and Romanet, p. 134). His sons, Charles Edward and Theodore, were involved in the business which was quite prosperous for many years. David Haviland died in 1879, and Charles and Theodore became partners. In 1891, however, Theodore left the company and formed his own business in 1892 under the name of "Theodore Haviland." Haviland and Company was continued by Charles. He died in 1921, and his son, George, carried on the business until 1930 when it closed due to bankruptcy. The company was reorganized after 1941 when Theodore's son, William, was able to obtain the rights to the old Haviland and Co. marks and models which had been sold in 1931. The Theodore Haviland Company in Limoges reverted to the name of Haviland and Company. William retired in 1957, and the company was carried on by his sons. They retired in 1972, and the management of the company was tuned over to the Cerabati group under the name of "Haviland SA." The company remains in business today. For a more complete discussion of the Haviland Company and the Theodore Haviland Company, see my book *Haviland Collectables and Objects of Art* (1984). The book also contains a detailed discussion of the many marks used by both firms. Those marks with their time periods of use have been reprinted here. Haviland & Co. Marks and Theodore Haviland Marks are shown in the same section and are sequentially numbered.

HAVILAND, FRANK

Frank Haviland was the youngest son of Charles Edward Haviland. He was an artist and operated his own decorating studio from about 1910 to 1924. He used various marks which included his full name. These marks are sometimes found on Haviland blanks.

HAVILAND, ROBERT

Robert Haviland was the grandson of Charles Field Haviland. He established his own porcelain company around 1924. He was not connected with Haviland and Company or Theodore Haviland. Also he did not become the successor to his grandfather's firm (see Charles Field Haviland). He did, however, purchase the Charles Field Haviland back mark from the Gérard and Abbot company (GDA) in 1941 which has been used by his company since that date (see Gérard, Dufraisseix, and Abbot). Robert Haviland was associated with Le Tanneur until about 1948, and with C. Parlon from 1949. The firm of Haviland and Parlon is currently in operation.

H & C

These initials, underscored with "LIMOGES," do not indicate a Haviland & Co. mark. The mark is possibly one used by Hinrichs & Co., who were New York based china importers. The same initials in a crown and shield type mark with "Limoges" and "Déposé" are shown for the Hinrichs Company circa the 1880s–1891 (Kovel, 1986, p. 115).

JOUHANNEAUD AND DUBOIS
This company was in business from the mid 1840s until the mid 1870s. The production was geared to art objects, and pieces were not always marked.

KLINGENBERG, A. (AK) (AKCD)
A. Klingenberg operated a Limoges factory and decorating studio from the 1880s until about 1910 (Wood, p.32). In the first edition, this company was identified as Kittel and Klingenberg. Subsequent research shows that "Kitel" Klingenberg (one person) was an exporter of china in Limoges (see Klingenberg, Kitel). Very little documentation has been found for Klingenberg. Serry Wood (1951) notes when writing about Limoges factories other than Haviland that "first mention should go to the A. Klingenberg pottery whose product and mark was very prevalent in the American market from 1880 to 1910" (p. 32). The only mark shown in Wood's book, however, is "AKCD," which is the same mark attributed to Charles Dwenger by Röntgen (p. 236 with the words "Carlsbad, Austria," instead of "Limoges, France"). Lesur and Tardy (p. 129) list Kitel Klingenberg Cie. as an exporter from 1867–1872, followed by Klingenberg associated with Leonard (P. Leonard?) in 1873, and then Klingenberg alone from 1883–1887. No marks are illustrated, however, by Lesur and Tardy.

White ware marks of "AK" over "D" are found in conjunction with decorating marks of "AK Limoges" as well as with "AKCD Limoges." D'Albis and Romanet (p. 157) mention a "Dwenger" as having had a decorating studio in Limoges during the early 1900s. Because the "AK Limoges" decorating mark is exactly the same style as the "AKCD" mark, the probability is that Klingenberg and Dwenger merged, or that Dwenger took over Klingenberg. The "AK" decorating marks should precede those of "AKCD," indicating Klingenberg decorating activities prior to his china production. One example has been found, however, which has the "AK" decorating mark on an "AK/D" blank, perhaps only indicating that the "AK" decorating mark was used for some time after the white ware mark changed to include "D" and before the "AKCD" decorating mark was instituted.

The general time period for the Klingenberg and Dwenger marks is probably early 1880s until 1910 or prior to World War I. The AKCD mark showing the Klingenberg and Dwenger association is listed here under Klingenberg as Mark 9.

A variety of finely decorated pieces carry the "AK" or "AKCD" marks. The decorating marks are found on white ware made by other Limoges factories. Examples also prove that the company supplied blanks for American china painters.

KLINGENBERG, KITEL
Kitel Klingenberg exported Limoges porcelain from the late 1860s until the early 1870s. (See Klingenberg, A.)

LANTERNIER, A. (AL)
The Lanternier family exported porcelain from Limoges during the 1850s. Some sources note the year 1855 as the beginning date of the Lanternier porcelain factory, but the company did not actually become engaged in manufacturing porcelain until the mid 1880s. The factory was started by A. Lanternier's father. The company carried on an extensive export trade with table china being its chief product. The white wares are often seen with the decorating mark of other companies or studios. While there are a number of marks found for the company, most seem to date circa 1900 and after, rather than the mid 1880s when the factory was first established. The marks carry the initial "A." for the son, Alfred, and not the initial "F." for the father. Mark 5 is the exception with only "Lanternier" in a circle without any initial. The company is still in operation.

LA PORCELAINE LIMOUSINE (PL)
This factory was the successor of the Barny, Rigoni, and Redon company, circa 1905 or 1906. The Redon mark (see Mark 4) was used on decorated ware. White wares carry either Mark 1, 2, or 3. Double marks indicate factory decoration, although white wares decorated by American china painters are more commonly seen. Table china and decorative accessories were produced. The company was in business until the late 1930s. (See Redon, M.)

LAPORTE, RAYMOND (RL)
Raymond Laporte was in business in Limoges from circa 1883 until 1897. Very few examples are found with the Laporte marks which were in the form of a butterfly. The piece shown with Laporte's mark here is on a cup and saucer. The scarcity of examples indicates that his production was not geared to export. The marks seem to indicate a change reflecting the U.S. tariff laws of 1890 as Mark 1 does not include "France."

LATRILLE FRÈRES
Latrille Frères was in operation from 1899 until 1913. The location of the factory was an old abbey which had been used for making porcelain by the Latrille brothers' father (d'Albis and Romanet, pp. 92; 240). D'Albis and Romanet (p. 92) also indicate that J. Granger joined the company in 1908 and stayed with the firm until 1913. In the first edition, the white ware mark used by Latrille Frères was listed as an unidentified Limoges mark. The "Old Abbey" decorating mark was also attributed to H. Créange, for according to Lesur and Tardy (1967, p. 111), Créange used the same mark. The mark, however, probably refers to the mark found on pieces exported or sold by Créange. He was listed as a *negociant*, and not actually a manufacturer. The "Old Abbey" mark has also been associated with J. Granger and seemingly reflects the time when he was associated with the Latrille factory. Another type of "Old Abbey" mark remains attributed to

Créange in this edition because that mark is in conjunction with the "HC" white ware mark (see Créange, H.).

Pieces found with the Old Abbey mark now attributed to Latrille Frères (Mark 3) usually have Mark 1 as the white ware mark. Mark 1 is also found alone or with the decorating mark of other Limoges factories. Mark 2 appears to be an early decorating mark for the company. It was probably used prior to Granger's association with the company. The mark was found on a piece of china originally exported to England, thus it is possible that Mark 2 was not used on china exported to America. Mark 3 is sometimes found without a white ware mark.

LAVIOLETTE

The Laviolette Company was in business from 1896–1905 (d'Albis and Romanet, p. 240). The mark used by this company, an arrow with "Limoges, France," was listed in the first edition as an unidentified Limoges mark. Examples always seem to have a decorating mark of some other company, or are examples of white ware decorated by American china painters.

LAZEYRAS, ROSENFELD, AND LEHMAN (LR&L)

This company was a decorating firm from all indications. Several decorating marks were used by the studio. The marks are found on expertly decorated game and fish services as well as figural and portrait plates and chargers. The company appears to have been the successor to the Th. Lazeyras firm, circa the 1920s. The LRL marks usually appear alone without any accompanying white ware mark. Two other marks shown in this edition are attributed to this company because the style of the marks and the initials are the same, except the last "L" is missing. The mark probably reflects the time when the third partner (Lehman) was not associated with the company. The particular pieces with these marks (see Marks 4 and 5) have the white ware mark used by J. Granger from 1922–1938. Thus the LR mark would have to be after 1922. The LR mark will remain under this company until information is found which might indicate that it belongs to another company or studio.

L. B. H.

These initials are found in an overglaze decorating mark of an unidentified studio. The few examples seen are on Coiffe blanks. The studio appears to have been in business during the 1890s.

LEGRAND, F.

F. Legrand was associated with Bétoule around 1910. The company manufactured table wares during the 1920s, but eventually the factory diverted its production to industrial porcelain manufacturing. Marks for the table china are circa the 1920s. Few examples are seen.

LEONARD, P. H. (PHL)

The P. H. Leonard Company was a New York based firm which imported porcelain from Germany and Limoges during the 1890s until the years of World War I. The P. H. Leonard mark was used instead of a Limoges factory decorating mark. The Leonard mark is often found with the Laviolette white ware mark. Pieces with the Leonard mark all seem to be factory or French studio decorated and not blanks decorated by American china painters.

LEVY (IMPERIAL)

The Imperial mark with a crown is attributed to Levy and Company. The mark appears as the decorating mark on pieces having white ware marks of other companies. Art objects and table china have been found with this mark. The time period for the mark would seem to be the late 1800s to the early 1900s, prior to World War I.

LIMOGES ART PORCELAINE CO.

This company is an unidentified decorating studio. The mark appeared on a pancake dish made by A. Lanternier, circa the early 1900s.

LIMOGES, FRANCE

"Limoges, France" with or without some symbol is found on many examples of Limoges porcelain. The companies using the various marks are unidentified. The majority of these marks are underglaze white ware marks. Often there is an identified company's decorating mark which can help indicate the time period when these several factories were in business. A few listed in this section in the first edition have now been identified, perhaps others will be in the future. (See Limoges, France Marks 1-9.)

MAAS, S.

S. Maas was in the porcelain business in Limoges during the 1890s. Few examples are found with the Maas mark.

MARTIN, CHARLES (CM)

Charles Martin was the successor to the Nivet Company during the 1880s. Martin was associated with several different people until about 1920 when Duché joined the company. White wares, table china, and art objects were produced until about the mid 1930s. The decorating marks for the company are similar to one white ware mark, a triangle with a "CM" monogram (see Marks 2 and 3). These marks appear to date from the early 1900s until the factory closed. Another white ware mark is attributed to the Martin Company (see Mark 1).

This mark is probably after 1891. It was used during the same period as decorating Mark 3 because pieces are found with both marks. The decorating mark may have either "DÉCOR," or "DÉPOSÉ" printed on one side of the triangle. "MARTIN" over "FRANCE" is sometimes found as an overglaze mark as well.

MAVALEIX, PAUL MAURICE (PM DE M)

P. M. Mavaleix was associated with Balleroy and Mandavy during the early 1900s. In 1908, he was in business by himself until about 1914. After World War I, circa 1920, J. Granger joined his company (d'Albis and Romanet, p. 170).

There has been some confusion about Mavaleix's white ware mark. The mark consists of a monogram incorporating the letters "PM DE M," which stand for Mavaleix's full name. The letter "P," however, clearly seems to be a "B" in the mark, at least on first inspection. Actually, it appears that the letter "P" merely has a fancy addition. Relatively few items are found with this mark. Most are white wares which have been decorated by other factories or studios, such as Borgfeldt (Coronet). No overglaze decorating mark has been noted for this company. A bees and hive decorating mark has been found on one example. That mark is unidentified, but it is doubtful that the mark can be attributed to Mavaleix. (See Granger, J. for this company and marks after World War I.)

MC. D. & S., J.

These initials are unidentified by specific name, but the company exported European and Japanese porcelain to the United States during the latter part of the nineteenth century. It was probably in business until World War I. The company either substituted or added its mark to china manufactured by Limoges factories. If there is a white ware mark in addition to the J. MC. D. & S. mark, it is probable that it was the factory which decorated the china.

MERLIN-LEMAS, P. (PML)

This company manufactured and decorated porcelain in Limoges during the 1920s. Only the white ware mark for this company is shown by other references. One example in the first edition carried the decorating mark as well (see Mark 2). Few examples, however, are found with the Merlin-Lemas marks.

M. F. & Co.

These initials were listed as belonging to an unidentified company in the first edition. The mark should be attributed to Marshall Field & Co., a Chicago based department store. Usually such store names were affixed as marks in addition to a factory decorating mark. In this case, the mark was ambiguous. Other marks on Limoges porcelain made for Marshall Field & Co. include the store's full name.

PAIRPOINT

The Pairpoint glass company of New Bedford, Massachusetts, decorated Limoges white wares. A special mark of "Pairpoint Limoges" is found on the examples decorated by the artists of that company. No white ware factory mark has been seen in conjunction with the Pairpoint decorating mark, thus the Limoges manufacturer of the porcelain remains unknown. It is possible that the company purchased blanks from several Limoges companies as was the practice of other American decorating studios. Pieces are expertly and richly decorated. They often command prices higher than comparable Limoges decorated pieces, due to the collectible nature of Pairpoint items in general.

PAROUTAUD FRÈRES (PP or P and P)

Paroutaud Frères manufactured white wares in the form of art objects and decorative accessories. Factory decorated pieces have not been seen, but a business card for the firm states that both whites wares and decorated china were produced. The company had three locations, two in Limoges and one in La Seynie. The marks incorporate both names. The company was in business from about 1903 until 1917.

PASTAUD, P.

The Pastaud company was a decorating studio operating in Limoges during the 1920s through the 1950s. P. Pastaud and Paul Pastaud as well as E. Pastaud and "Pataud" (probably misspelled) are listed by Lesur and Tardy (1967, pp. 140, 141) as being decorators at the same locations during those years. Presumably P. and Paul were the same person. Examples decorated by the company were evidently not intended for export to the United States as examples are rarely found. The piece shown in the photographs is of a vase exhibiting very fine workmanship, highly decorated with gold paste work and enamelling.

PILLIVUYT, A.

This company was in business from about 1913 until 1936 (d'Albis and Romanet, p. 241). The mark shown in this edition was used during the 1920s.

PLAINEMAISON

The Plainemaison Company was in business from circa the 1890s until about 1910. Few example are found with the factory's mark. It appears that only white wares were produced. Examples have all been decorated by American china painters or French decorating studios.

POUYAT, JEAN (JP)

The Pouyat family was one of the oldest French names connected with the Limoges porcelain industry. Jean Pouyat's grandfather had a faience factory in the 1760s at St. Yrieix. He also owned kaolin mines in that area in the late 1700s. Jean's father, François, operated a hard paste porcelain factory in Paris from the early 1800s until around 1840. Jean Pouyat established a company circa 1842 at Limoges. Jean died in 1849, and the business was carried on by his sons. Circa 1883 the company was known as La Céramique. The Pouyat company was joined with the firm of William Guérin a few years before World War I, ca. 1911. (See Guérin, W.)

Wares manufactured by the Pouyat firm represent another of the most visible Limoges companies on the American antiques market today. The company carried on a large export trade during the late 1800s with the United States. Examples of Pouyat marked porcelain range from white wares and table china to factory decorated art objects and accessories. Double marks indicate that the items were factory decorated. Additional marks such as "Handpainted," or "Peint et Doré a la main a Limoges" may appear with the marks. The company was particularly famous for its white wares or "blanks." Wood (1951, p. 31) mentions that the company did not produce factory decorated dinner services until after 1890.

The earliest marks attributed to the company date from the 1850s (see Marks 1 and 2). D'Albis and Romanet (p. 241) show Mark 3 in use about 1876. A similar decorating mark is found printed in red with "Décor" above the initials (see Mark 4). Mark 3 (white ware) and Mark 4 should date during the same time period, from about 1876 to 1890. Mark 6 is like Mark 4 except "France" has been added to it, indicating a date after 1890. It is the same type of mark as Mark 5 which is a white ware mark. While Mark 5 appears to be the only white ware mark used after 1890, the decorating Marks show some changes. Mark 4 was probably used only a short time. Few examples are found with this mark. Mark 7 is seen more frequently; "France" is not part of that mark, but it was probably in use after Mark 6, perhaps until the company was combined with Guérin or until World War I. Wood (p. 34) shows that mark to have been in use in 1900. Marks 8 and 9 are later decorating marks, probably after World War I. Although d'Albis and Romanet (p. 241) show Mark 8 in use from 1890 to 1932, examples seen to indicate a later time than 1890. Marks 5, 8, and 9 are the most frequently seen Pouyat marks.

When the Guérin firm became a part of Bawo and Dotter after World War I, the Pouyat marks continued to be used until the Bawo and Dotter company closed about 1932. (See Guérin, Wm.; Bawo & Dotter.)

RAYNAUD, M. (R&CO.)

Martial Raynaud had been connected with the Limoges porcelain industry during the early 1900s, and the year 1911 is usually associated with his marks. Two of his early marks included a chicken in one and a duck in another. Examples with these marks have not surfaced. Marks 1 and 2 are the ones most commonly seen. These marks date from after the time Raynaud took over the Vogt firm (see Tressemann & Vogt), circa 1919. The T&V "Bell" mark was continued by Raynaud; however, when the Bell mark was used by Raynaud, it seems to have been in conjunction with his initials as shown in Mark 2. Sometimes the T&V white ware mark may be found on pieces with Mark 2. This probably indicates that existing white ware stock already marked was used and does not mean that he continued to use a T&V white ware mark. The Raynaud Marks shown here do not appear to have been used after World War II. Objects having the R&Co. mark and the T&V Bell mark are later than pieces having only the original T&V Bell mark. The Raynaud Company remains in business today, under the name of Raynaud's son, André.

REDON, M. (MR)

Martial Redon was involved in the Limoges porcelain industry from the early 1850s (see Gibus and Redon). Redon's marks, however, date from the early 1880s, reflecting the time when Gibus left the company. White wares, table china, decorative accessories, and art objects were manufactured. Factory decorated pieces are not always double marked. Redon died in 1890, but the company and its marks were continued by Redon's son until about 1896 (d'Albis and Romanet, p. 130). For Redon marks after 1902, see Barny and Rigoni and La Porcelaine Limousine.

ROYAL CHINA

The mark "Royal China, Limoges" with a crown is found as an overglaze decorating mark in red. The studio is unidentified. The mark was found on a Granger blank, and consequently the mark is after 1922.

SAZERAT, LEON AND BLONDEAU

Leon Sazerat began his career in the Limoges porcelain industry during the 1850s. He was associated with Blondeau from the early 1880s. Mark 1 is found on white ware, and Mark 3 is on factory decorated china. Both of these marks seem to reflect the time of the company after Sazerat's death, however, in 1891. Mark 1 includes "FRANCE," (used after 1891), and Mark 3 includes the names of Blondeau's partners after Sazerat died, Pichonnier and Duboucheron (d'Albis and Romanet, p. 132). That company continued until the late 1890s. Mark 2 would have been used prior to 1891.

SERPAUT, CHARLES

Charles Serpaut had worked for Bernardaud before establishing his own company about 1920 (d'Albis and Romanet, p. 115). The factory was continued by his son until the late 1950s. The mark on examples shown, however, is prior to World War II, ca. the 1920s–1930s. A printed overglaze full name mark was used after that time. Another mark, containing the initials "B. S." in a star was found as a decorating mark with the Serpaut white ware mark. No information has been found, however, to connect that particular mark to the Serpaut factory. (See this mark under "B. S.")

STRAUS, LEWIS AND SONS (LS&S)

Lewis Straus and Sons exported porcelain from Austria and Limoges to their New York based company from the 1890s until circa the mid 1920s. The Straus mark is found as an overglaze mark on factory decorated items. Often there is a white ware mark of the Limoges manufacturing company, such as Coiffe, but sometimes pieces are marked only with the Straus mark. Blanks painted by American china painters, however, are not found. Pieces are always professionally decorated, often handpainted and signed by French artists.

SW

These initials with "BIARRITZ" were found with a wreath as an overglaze decorating mark in red. The decorating studio is unidentified. The "SW" mark was on a piece of white ware with unidentified Limoges, France Mark 4. From the example, the time when the "SW" mark was used would be circa the late 1800s, after 1891.

TEISSONNIÈRE, JULES

This firm was in business from about 1908 until the 1940s. White wares and decorative accessories were manufactured.

TÉXERAUD, LÉON

This company was in operation during the 1920s. Table china and decorative accessories were manufactured by the factory. Note that Mark 1 does not contain the work "Elite" as it is sometimes mistaken to be. The letters are the French spelling for Téxeraud's initials.

THARAUD, C.

This company was in business from about 1920 until the late 1960s.

TOUZE, LEMAÎTRE FRÈRES & BLANCHER (TLB)

This company was formed after World War I, succeeding an older Touze factory originally established about 1901. The TLB factory was in business until the late 1930s. Pieces made by this company are not frequently seen. The mark is unusual as it is in the form of a chicken. A mark of "Limoges, France, Unique" was also used by the company. A very striking Art Deco coffee set has been seen with Mark 1. This set was not an export item and did not carry a decorating mark.

TRESSEMANN (or TRESSEMANES) & VOGT (T&V)

Tressemann and Vogt became partners in the porcelain decorating and exporting business in Limoges during the early 1880s. Vogt's father had started a company in Limoges in the 1850s for exporting and later decorating china to be shipped to his New York based company (see Vogt, John). The T&V firm did not start manufacturing porcelain until 1891 (d'Albis and Romanet, p. 155). The partnership lasted sixteen years, until 1907. After that time, the company was known as Porcelaine Gustave Vogt until about 1919 when it was sold to Martial Raynaud.

Mark 1 appears to be perhaps the earliest mark used by T&V. It is in blue and contains both partners' names. Mark 2 is an early decorating mark. It is a "Bell" without "France" as part of the mark. Mark 3 is another decorating mark which is seldom seen. It is a rose or flower shape with " T&V" and "France," and would date after 1891. Marks 1–3 were probably all used before the company manufactured any porcelain. The distinctive "Bell" mark changed design after 1907 when the company became "Porcelaine Gustave Vogt" (see Marks 14–16). The later "Bell" was continued by Vogt's successor, Raynaud, but Raynaud's marks also include his initials (see Raynaud, M.).

It seems that the New York based firm of Vogt and Dose probably decorated some of the T&V production. No information has been found to indicate whether the New York company marked its pieces with a decorating mark or not. Some decorating marks are seldom seen, such as Mark 3 and Marks 12–15. D'Albis and Romanet (p. 156) indicate that the Vogt and Dose company in New York closed about 1931 because the imported china from France and Germany was arriving already decorated and "the situation of the decorators had become very precarious." This statement implies that a New York studio had been engaged in decorating porcelain for a long time, including periods both before and after the T&V factory was in operation.

The white ware marks used by T&V are somewhat easier to date because none can be prior to 1891. Although Mark 4a does not incorporate "France," it was still not used before 1891. (Perhaps some other Limoges factory producing the china marked the pieces for T&V, but there is no proof of this.) Mark 4 was probably the first white ware mark used by the T&V factory. A number of variations of the same mark are found (see Marks 5–7). Mark 8 with "Déposé," is similar to the one shown by d'Albis and Romanet (p. 242) which they date after 1907 until 1919 when Raynaud took over the company. D'Albis and Romanet, however, also indicate that these same marks were continued by Raynaud. Examples, however, show that Raynaud also included his initials with the "Bell" mark or used his initials as a white ware mark. Some examples do have one of the T&V white ware marks and a Raynaud decorating mark. This probably means that Raynaud merely added his decorating mark to existing white ware stock already marked with " T&V" before he took over the company. Thus T&V white ware marks would not have been used after 1919 unless a Raynaud mark accompanies them as an overglaze decorating mark.

Mark 9 is an overglaze decorating Mark in purple with "France." It is not seen often, and it may appear with the white ware mark of another factory. It should date after 1891, circa the early 1890s. Decorating Mark 10 (red "Bell" with "Limoges") was found with white ware Mark 6, indicating a date of circa 1900. Mark 11 (red "Bell" with "France") is the most commonly found T&V decorating mark. It was probably used during the latter part of the 1891–1907 period.

Marks 12–15 are decorating marks which seem to have been used when Vogt took over the company after 1907. These are rarely seen. Mark 16 is the most common decorating mark found for the 1907–1919 era. Sometimes Mark 16 is found with T&V white ware Marks 4–7, rather that Mark 8. The explanation is that the white wares were not decorated until a later time, after the decorating marks had changed.

A large percentage of available Limoges porcelain carries the T&V marks. From the decoration, it is obvious that a lot of the production was exported as blanks and decorated by amateur American china painters. The T&V decorating mark is also found on china with other Limoges factories' white ware marks, indicating that the piece was decorated by T&V, but not made by the company. The studio or factory decorated pieces are the most desirable.

The Smithsonian Institute's Museum of History and Technology has the State china used by President Benjamin Harrison which was made and decorated by T&V in 1892. The back marks are 5a (white ware) and 10 (decorating mark in gold).

UNION CÉRAMIQUE (UC)
Union Céramique was in business from about 1909 until 1938. Table wares are sometimes found with the factory's marks.

UNION LIMOUSINE (UL)
This company appears to have been in business from about 1908, and it is still in operation today. Very few examples are found with the factory's marks. The mark shown here is circa the 1930s–1950s.

V. F.
These initials with "FRANCE," surrounded by small stars are found as a white ware mark of an unidentified company. It is not a mark of Vignaud Frères. The time period when this mark was in use would be the early 1900s.

VIGNAUD FRÈRES
Vignaud Frères was established in 1911 and was in business until 1938. White wares and factory decorated table china were produced.

VILLEGOUREIX, NOEL & CIE.
This company was in business from about 1919 until the mid 1920s. Few examples are found with the mark, an elaborate letter "V" in a fancy shield.

VOGT, JOHN
John Vogt was involved in the china importing business in New York during the 1840s. Later, in the early 1850s he established an exporting firm at Limoges, and in the 1860s he also opened a decorating studio at Limoges. In the early 1870s, John's son, Gustave, took over the Limoges operation (see Tressemanes & Vogt). The New York company continued from the mid 1860s until 1931 under the name of Vogt and Dose. The New York company sold imported china, and also had a decorating studio from the mid 1860s until 1931 (d'Albis and Romanet, pp. 155, 156).

VULTURY FRÈRES
This factory was in business from about 1887 until 1904. Examples with their mark, a bird with "LIMOGES, FRANCE," are rarely seen. The mark used by this company is not the same as unidentified LIMOGES, FRANCE Mark 7.

WANAMAKER'S
In the first edition, an overglaze mark of the letter "W" in a wreath was shown as an unidentified company. The mark can be attributed to Wanamaker's, a Philadelphia based department store which imported Limoges china.

ALPHABETICAL LISTING OF MARKS FOR LIMOGES FACTORIES AND STUDIOS

The marks shown in this section correspond to the factories and studios listed in the preceding section. Please note, however, that marks are not shown for every company listed. The marks are numbered only within each company and not sequentially. For example, Bernardaud & Co., Mark 1, B&CO. Mark 2, B&CO. Mark 3; E. G. D. & Co.; Guérin, W. & Co., Mark 1, Guérin Mark 2, Guérin Mark 3, etc. Consult the Index and Cross Reference To Companies, Initials, and Symbols if a particular mark is not found.

Please note that in several cases, the photographs of marks contain more than one mark, usually the underglaze white ware mark and the overglaze decorating mark. Because often both marks were close together, it was not possible to photograph only one mark. Refer to the caption to determine which one is the specific mark for that particular caption.

A & D, Limoges, France, overglaze decorating Mark in red or green, unidentified studio, ca. late 1800s.

Ahrenfeldt, Charles, overglaze decorating Mark in red, ca. 1884 to 1893.

Ahrenfeldt, Charles J., Mark 1, overglaze decorating mark in blue, CA monogram with "Limoges, France," ca. after 1893.

Ahrenfeldt, Charles J., Mark 2, underglaze white ware Mark in green, CA monogram, ca. after 1894 to 1930s.

Ahrenfeldt, Charles J., Mark 3, underglaze white ware Mark in green, CA monogram with a star and "France," ca. after 1894-1930s.

Ahrenfeldt, Charles J., Mark 4, underglaze white ware Mark in green, CA monogram with "France," ca. after 1894-1930s.

Ahrenfeldt, Charles J., Mark 5, underglaze white ware Mark in green, CA monogram with star and zig-zag lines, ca. after 1894-1930s.

Ahrenfeldt, Charles J., Mark 6, underglaze white ware Mark in green, CA monogram with "France, Déposé," ca. after 1894-1930s.

Ahrenfeldt, Charles J., Mark 7, overglaze decorating Mark in green, CA monogram in a double circle with "Limoges, France," ca. after 1894-1930s.

Ahrenfeldt, Charles J., Mark 8a, overglaze decorating Mark in green or gold, "C. Ahrenfeldt, Limoges," ca. after 1894-1930s.

Ahrenfeldt, Charles J., Mark 8b, variation of Mark 8a, overglaze decorating Mark in green, "Made by C. Ahrenfeldt, Limoges," with importer's name, ca. after 1894-1930.

Ahrenfeldt, Charles J., Mark 9, overglaze decorating Mark in blue (incorporating Mark 5), ca. after World War II until 1969.

AJCO, unidentified decorating studio, overglaze monogram Mark in blue, ca. 1930s or later.

Alluaud, François II, Mark 1, "FA," ca. before 1876.

Alluaud, Mark 2, "AF," ca. before 1876.

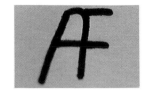

Alluaud, Mark 3, "AF" monogram, ca. before 1876.

Aluminite, "FRG, Limoges, France," ca. 1920s.

Ardant, Henri, bird on a branch, ca. 1859 to early 1880s.

A V, impressed Mark, unidentified factory, possibly Aragon and Vultury, ca. 1880s.

Balleroy, H., Mark 1, underglaze white ware Mark in green, ca. 1908-late 1930s.

Balleroy, H., Mark 2, overglaze decorating Mark, ca. 1908-late 1930s.

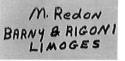

Barny and Rigoni, Mark 1, "Limoges, France" printed in flag design, ca. 1894-1902.

Barny, Rigoni, and Redon, Mark 2, ca. 1902-1904.

Barny, Rigoni, & Langle, Mark 3, underglaze white ware Mark in green, ca. 1904-1906.

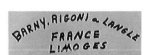

Barny, Rigoni, & Langle, Mark 4, overglaze decorating Mark, ca. 1904-1906.

Bassett, overglaze import Mark in red or green, ca. late 1800s-1914.

Bawo & Dotter, Mark 1, early overglaze decorating Mark in green, bottle shape with Arms of Limoges (worn in this example) and "Limoges" printed underneath, ca. 1870s-1880s.

Bawo & Dotter, Mark 2, early decorating Mark in red, like Mark 1, ca. 1870s-1880s.

Bawo & Dotter, Mark 3, early decorating Mark in red, like Marks 1 and 2 plus the initials "B. D." and "L.," ca. 1880s.

Bawo & Dotter, Mark 4, underglaze white ware Mark in green with "Limoges" written in script, ca. 1896-1900.

ELITE
L
FRANCE

Bawo & Dotter, Mark 5, underglaze white ware Mark in green, "ELITE/L/FRANCE," ca. after 1900.

Bawo & Dotter, Mark 6, overglaze decorating Mark in red, without "France," ca. 1880s-1891.

Bawo & Dotter, Mark 7, underglaze white ware Mark in green or overglaze decorating Mark in red, usually seen in conjuction with an American retailer's mark, ca. 1896-1900.

Bawo & Dotter, Mark 8, overglaze decorating Mark in red with "Limoges" written in script, and "France" printed, ca. 1896-1900.

Bawo & Dotter, Mark 9, overglaze decorating Mark in red with "ELITE WORKS," ca. 1900-1914.

Bawo & Dotter, Mark 10, overglaze decorating Mark in red, wreath with "ELITE" printed in center and "HAND PAINTED" printed in ribbon on either side of wreath, ca. 1900-1914.

Bawo & Dotter, Mark 11, overglaze decorating Mark in red with "ELITE" printed above Arms and "LIMOGES" printed below, ca. 1920-1932.

Bawo & Dotter, Mark 12, overglaze decorating Mark in black and brown, "Guérin, Pouyat, Elite, Ltd.," printed inside ornate emblem, ca. after 1920.

Beaux-Arts, overglaze decorating Mark in green with "FRENCH CHINA," ca. 1900.

Bernardaud & Co., Mark 1, underglaze white ware Mark in green, "B&CO." over "FRANCE," ca. 1900-1914.

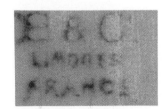

Bernardaud & Co., Mark 2, underglaze white ware Mark in green, "B&CO." over "LIMOGES, FRANCE," ca. 1914-1930s and after.

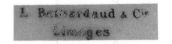

Bernardaud & Co., Mark 3, overglaze decorating Mark in red "L. Bernardaud & Cie.," ca. 1900-1930s and after.

B. H., underglaze white ware Mark in green, unidentified factory, ca. 1920s.

B. & H. overglaze decorating Mark in green, gray, or red, unidentified decorating studio, ca. 1890s.

Blakeman & Henderson, overglaze decorating Mark in green, ca. 1890s.

Boisbertrand, "LIMOGES" printed inside banner, ca. late 1920s.

Borgfeldt, George (Coronet), Mark 1, overglaze decorating Mark in green or blue, crown with "CORONET," ca. 1906-1920.

Borgfeldt, Mark 2, overglaze decorating Mark in green like Mark 1 but with "TRADE MARK," after 1920.

Boyer, Jean, Mark 1, underglaze white ware Mark in green, ca. 1919-mid 1930s.

Boyer, Jean, Mark 2, overglaze decorating Mark in blue, ca. 1919-mid 1930s.

B. S., overglaze decorating Mark in green, unidentified decorating studio, ca. 1920s.

C. et J., overglaze decorating Mark in red, ca. late 1800s-1914.

C. H., underglaze white ware Mark in green with Arms of Limoges and "DÉPOSÉ," ca. 1880s-1890.

Chabrol Frères & Poirer, wings and star Mark, ca. 1920s.

Chauffraisse, Rougerie, & Co., "L. Hermitage," Mark with "CR," ca. late 1920s.

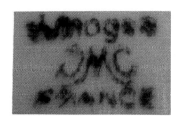

CMC or GMC, underglaze white ware Mark in green, ca. after 1890-1914.

Coiffe, Mark 1, underglaze white ware Mark in green without "FRANCE," ca. before 1890.

Coiffe, Mark 2, underglaze white ware Mark in green with "FRANCE," ca. after 1891-1914.

Coiffe, Mark 3, underglaze white ware Mark in green with "LIMOGES, FRANCE," ca. after 1891-1914.

Coiffe, Mark 4, underglaze white ware Mark in green with "MADE IN FRANCE," after 1914-1920s.

Comte D'Artois, overglaze decal Mark in blue, ca. late 20th century.

Créange, Henri, Mark 1, underglaze white ware Mark in green, ca. 1907-1914.

Créange, Mark 2, overglaze decorating Mark in black and gold, crossed swords and wreath, ca. 1907-1914.

Délinières, R., (D&CO.), Mark 1, underglaze white ware Mark in green, ca. 1870s.

D&CO., Mark 2, underglaze white ware Mark in green with one line under initials, ca. 1879-1893.

D&CO., Mark 3, underglaze white ware Mark in green with "FRANCE," ca. 1894-1900.

D&CO., Mark 4, overglaze decorating Mark in red, pot or vase design, ca. 1881-1893.

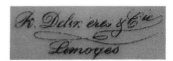

D&CO., Mark 5, overglaze decorating Mark in red, name written in script form, ca. 1894-1900.

D&CO., Mark 6, overglaze decorating Mark in red, printed name in oval shape with name of Scottish importer.

Demartine, G., Mark 1, underglaze white ware Mark in green, initials with "Limoges, France," ca. after 1891 to early 1900s.

Demartine, Mark 2, overglaze decorating Mark in blue-green with "Avenir" printed inside a circle, ca. after 1891 to early 1900s.

E. G. D. & CO., overglaze decorating Mark in green, ca. 1890s.

Flambeau China (LDB&C), Mark 1, underglaze white ware Mark in green, torch with "Limoges, France," ca. 1890s-1914.

Flambeau China, Mark 2, overglaze decorating Mark in red, torch with initials and "Limoges, France," ca. 1890s, probably used before the company manufactured porcelain.

Flambeau China, Mark 3, overglaze decorating Mark in green, red, or blue with "Flambeau," ca. 1890s to early 1900s.

Flambeau China, Mark 4, overglaze decorating Mark in green with "Flambeau, Limoges, France" printed in banner around torch with "Hand Painted," ca. 1890s to early 1900s.

Flambeau China, Mark 5, overglaze decorating Mark in green, torch in oval shape with initials and "Flambeau China," ca. before 1914 and after Marks 2, 3, and 4.

Flambeau China, Mark 6, overglaze decorating Mark in green, initials and "Flambeau China" printed in circular design around torch with "Hand Painted," ca. before 1914, and after Marks 2, 3, and 4.

Florale, overglaze decorating Mark in green, ca. 1920s.

Fontanille and Marraud (FM), Mark 1, after 1935.

Fontanille and Marraud, Mark 2, "Porcelaine Artistique," after 1935.

Fontanille and Marraud, Mark 3, "Porcelaine Artistique," with "Barbotine" and "Grand Feu," after 1935.

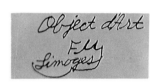

Fontanille and Marraud, Mark 4, "Object d'Art," after 1935.

François, André, underglaze white ware Mark in green, ca. after 1919 to mid 1930s.

Gérard, Dufraisseix, and Abbot (GDA), Mark 1, underglaze white ware Mark in green, ca. 1900-1941.

Gérard, Dufraisseix, and Abbot, Mark 2, underglaze white ware Mark in green, "Porcelaine de Feu," ca. early 1900s.

Gérard, Dufraisseix, and Abbot, Mark 3, overglaze decorating Mark in red, "CH. FIELD HAVILAND" printed inside double circle, ca. 1900-1941.

Gérard, Dufraisseix, and Abbot, Mark 4, overglaze decorating Mark in red or green, ca. after 1941 to present.

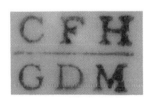

Gérard, Dufraisseix, and Morel (GDM), Mark 1, underglaze white ware Mark in green, ca. 1882-1890.

Gérard, Dufraisseix, and Morel, Mark 2, underglaze white ware Mark in green with "FRANCE," ca. after 1891-1900.

Gérard, Dufraisseix, and Morel, Mark 3, overglaze decorating Mark in red, blue, grey, brown, or black "CH. FIELD HAVILAND" printed inside double circle, ca. 1882-1900.

Gibus and Redon, Mark 1, incised initials, ca. 1872-1881.

Gibus and Redon, Mark 2, overglaze decorating Mark in red, prior to 1882.

Giraud, A., underglaze white ware Mark in green, ca. 1920s.

Granger, J., Mark 1, underglaze white ware Mark in green, GM monogram with "LIMOGES FRANCE," ca. 1922-1938.

Granger, Mark 2, underglaze white ware Mark in green, GM monogram with "FRANCE, DÉPOSÉ," ca. 1922-1938.

Guérin, William, Mark 1, underglaze white ware Mark in green, "W G & Ce," ca. 1870s.

Guérin, Mark 2, underglaze white ware Mark in green, "WG & Co. FRANCE," before 1891-1900.

Guérin, Mark 3, underglaze white ware Mark in green, with "LIMOGES" and "FRANCE," ca. after 1900-1932.

Guérin, Mark 4, overglaze decorating Mark in red, blue, green, brown, or gold, ca. late 1800s to 1932.

Gutherz, Oscar, overglaze decorating Mark in red, ca. late 1800s.

Haviland and Abbot, overglaze importing Mark in red, ca. after 1886.

Haviland, Charles Field, Mark 1, impressed initials "CFH" on white ware, ca. after 1868-1881.

Haviland, Charles Field, Mark 2, underglaze white ware Mark in green, "CFH," ca. after 1868-1881.

Haviland, Charles Field, Mark 3, overglaze decorating Mark in black, brown, or blue, ca. after 1859-1881.

Haviland, Charles Field, Mark 4, "PORCELAINES A FEU," stamped on white ware in black, after 1868-1881.

Haviland, David (H&Co., Marks 1-22); Theodore Haviland (TH, Marks 23-35) Mark 1. Applied mark of impressed name, indicates pieces made for Haviland Bros. by other Limoges companies, but presumably decorated by the Haviland studio, early 1850s to about 1865.

Haviland & Co., Mark 2., Applied mark of impressed name, similar to Mark 1, early 1850s to about 1865.

Haviland & Co., Mark 3,
Applied mark of impressed
name with "Déposé," similar to
Marks 1 and 2, mid 1850s to
about 1865.

Haviland & Co., Mark 4,
Impressed name, not attached,
but impressed directly into
base, mid 1850s to about 1865.

Haviland & Co., Mark 5,
Impressed initials, used during
first period of porcelain
manufacture by Haviland &
Cie., 1865-1875.

Haviland & Co., Mark 6,
Underglaze initials in green,
1876-1880.

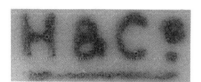

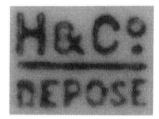

Haviland & Co., Mark 7,
Underglaze initials in green,
underscored. 1876-1880.

Haviland & Co., Mark 8, Underglaze initials
in green, underscored
with two lines, 1876-
1880.

Haviland & Co., Mark 9, Underglaze
intials in green, underscored with "L"
added to indicate "Limoges," 1876-1889.
Note: this same mark was used overglaze
as a decorating mark in various colors for a
short time from about 1878.

Haviland & Co., Mark 10,
Underglaze initials in green,
underscored with "Déposé,"
adopted about 1887.

Haviland & Co., Mark 11, Underglaze,
initials in green with
"L" for "Limoges" and
"FRANCE," 1888-
1896.

Haviland & Co., Mark 12,
Underglaze, full name with
"France," in green, 1893-1930.

Haviland & Co., Mark 13,
Overglaze full name with
"Limoges" in red, 1876-1930.
Note: presence of an overglaze
mark indicates factory
decoration.

Haviland & Co., Mark 14, Same as
Mark 13, in blue, 1876-1930. "Feu de
Four" added to indicate special firing
technique. Red overglaze mark
indicates pieces were made for the "R.
B. Gray Co., St. Louis," Missouri.

Haviland & Co., Mark 15, Overglaze in
red, importer mark of "Davis, Collamore, &
Co., Importers, 24.7 Broadway, New York."
Also impressed English Registry Mark,
indicating particular design had been
registered with the English Registry Office.

Haviland & Co., Mark 16,
Overglaze in blue, full name, 1876-
1878.

Haviland & Co., Mark 17, Overglaze,
in blue (or other
colors) double circle
mark with full name.
1879-1889.

Haviland & Co., Mark 18, Overglaze, in green,
same as Mark 17, 1879-
1889.

Haviland & Co., Mark 19, Round paper label with initials over "Elite" in green, 1878-1883. This mark was used to grade the whiteware, but it is overglaze. Another similar mark of "Special" under "H & Co" in reddish-brown was used at the same time. It is extremely rare to find examples with these paper marks.

Haviland & Co., Mark 20, Impressed full name underscored with "Limoges," art pottery mark, 1873-1882.

Haviland & Co., Mark 21, Impressed initials, art pottery mark, 1873-1882. Also paper label for *L'Escalier de Cristal*, exclusive outlet for the Haviland art pottery.

Haviland & Co., Mark 22, Impressed initials on stoneware with Chaplet's artist mark symbolizing a rosary, 1882-1886.

Theodore Haviland, Mark 23, Overglaze decorating mark, initials, in red, before 1892.

Theodore Haviland, Mark 24, Underglaze, in green, "Mont-Mery" over three castle towers, initials, "FRANCE," ca. 1892.

Theodore Haviland, Mark 25, Underglaze, in green, "TH. HAVILAND" over three castle towers. "Limoges" in script. "FRANCE" printed, ca. early 1890s (probably after 1892).

Theodore Haviland, Mark 26, Underglaze, in green, "Theo. Haviland," with "Limoges" in script, "FRANCE" printed, ca. 1893.

Theodore Haviland, Mark 27, Impressed intials with the Legion of Honor symbol, primary whiteware mark used to identify factory from 1894 to 1957.

Theodore Haviland, Mark 28, Impressed full name with "Theodore" underscored, the same design as overglaze Mark 34, ca. 1904 to mid 1920s.

Theodore Haviland, Mark 29, Underglaze, full name written in horseshoe shape, with "FRANCE" in center of mark, in green, ca. 1920-1936.

Theodore Haviland, Mark 30, Underglaze, full name with "FRANCE" in shield shape with "Limoges" in rectangular shape above, ca. 1936-1945.

Theodore Haviland, Mark 31, Overglaze, in green, initials with "Porcelaine Mousseline" separated by Legion of Honor symbol and "FRANCE," in circular shape, 1894-1903. Mark also was written horizontally with "Limoges" in script form under the initial "T." and "FRANCE" printed under the initial "H." 1894-1903.

Theodore Haviland, Mark 32, Overglaze, in red, full name with the Legion of Honor symbol (may appear with "Theodore" abbreviated to "Théo."). 1895 to probably 1903.

Theodore Haviland, Mark 33, Overglaze, in red, full name in printed script, slanted, with "Limoges" in written script, and "FRANCE" printed, 1903-1925.

Theodore Haviland, Mark 34, Overglaze, in red, same as in Mark 33, except "Theodore" is underscored, c. 1904 to mid 1920s.

Theodore Haviland, Mark 35, Overglaze, in red, similar to Marks 33 and 34, except the name is written with the letters straight aligned rather than slanted, 1925 to probably mid 1940s.

Haviland, Frank, Mark 1, overglaze decorating Mark in red, ca. 1910-1924.

Haviland, Frank, Mark 2, overglaze decorating Mark in red, variation of Mark 1, ca. 1910-1924.

Haviland, Robert, Mark 1, underglaze white ware Mark in green or overglaze decorating Mark, after 1924.

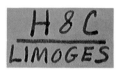

Haviland, Robert and Le Tanneur, Mark 2, overglaze Mark in brown, ca. late 1920s-1948.

Haviland, Robert, Mark 3, overglaze decorating Mark in red, "CH. FIELD HAVILAND" in double circle, after 1941.

Haviland, Robert and C. Parlon, Mark 4, overglaze decorating Mark, ca. after 1949.

H & C, underglaze white ware Mark in green with one line and "LIMOGES," (not a Haviland mark, company is possibly Hinrichs), ca. 1880s-1891.

AK

Klingenberg, A., Mark 1, overglaze decorating Mark in red, wine glass with initials, ca. early 1880s.

Klingenberg, Mark 2, overglaze decorating Mark in red, initials in circle, ca. 1880s-1890s.

Klingenberg, Mark 3, impressed or underglaze white ware Mark in green, "AK," ca. 1880s-1890.

Klingenberg, Mark 4, underglaze white ware Mark in green, initials with "FRANCE," ca. after 1891.

Klingenberg, Mark 5, underglaze white ware Mark in green, initials underscored with "FRANCE," ca. 1890s.

Klingenberg, Mark 6, underglaze white ware Mark in green, "AK" over "D," (showing Dwenger association), ca. 1890s-1910 but after Mark 5.

Klingenberg, Mark 7, underglaze white ware Mark in green, "AK" over "D," with "FRANCE," ca. 1890s-1910.

Klingenberg, Mark 8, underglaze white ware Mark in green "AK" over "D," underscored with "FRANCE," ca. 1890s-1910.

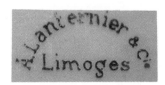

Klingenberg and Dwenger, Mark 9, overglaze decorating Mark in red "AKCD," ca. 1900-1910.

Lanternier, A., Mark 1, overglaze decorating Mark in red, full name with "Limoges," ca. 1890s.

Lanternier, Mark 2, underglaze white ware Mark in green, "A. L. DÉPOSÉ," ca. 1890s.

Lanternier, Mark 3, underglaze white ware Mark in green with anchor and "DÉPOSÉ," ca. 1890s.

Lanternier, Mark 4, underglaze white ware Mark in geen with anchor and "LIMOGES, FRANCE," ca. 1891-1914.

Lanternier, Mark 5, overglaze exporting or decorating Mark in blue, "LANTERNIER" printed inside double circle without initial "A.," ca. before 1890.

Lanternier, Mark 6, overglaze decorating Mark in red, brown, or blue double circle, ca. 1891-1914.

Lanternier, Mark 7, overglaze decorating Mark in red and black, wreath and shield, ca. after World War I.

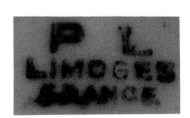

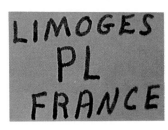

La Porcelaine Limousine (PL), Mark 1, underglaze white ware Mark in green, initials underscored with "LIMOGES, FRANCE," ca. 1905-late 1930s.

La Porcelaine Limousine, Mark 2, underglaze white ware Mark in green, like Mark 1 without line, ca. 1905-late 1930s.

La Porcelaine Limousine, Mark 3, underglaze white ware Mark in green, with "LIMOGES" above initials and "FRANCE" below, ca. 1905-late 1930s.

La Porcelaine Limousine, Mark 4, overglaze decorating Mark in red, "M. REDON" in circle (used with one of the PL white ware marks), ca. 1905-late 1930s.

Laporte, Raymond, Mark 1, butterfly with initials "RL/L," ca. 1883-1890.

Laporte, Raymond, Mark 2, overglaze decorating Mark in red, butterfly or insect with initials and "LIMOGES FRANCE," ca. 1891-1897.

Latrille Frères, Mark 1, underglaze white ware Mark in green, star with "LIMOGES FRANCE," ca. 1899-1913.

Latrille Frères, Mark 2, overglaze decorating Mark in red, ca. 1899-1908, probably toward end of period.

Latrille Frères, Mark 3, overglaze decorating Mark in green, "OLD ABBEY," ca. 1908-1913.

Laviolette, underglaze white ware Mark in green, arrow with "LIMOGES, FRANCE," ca. 1896-1905.

Lazeyras, Rosenfeld, and Lehman (LR&L), Mark 1, overglaze decorating Mark in red or blue, ca. 1920s.

Lazeyras, Rosenfeld, and Lehman, Mark 2, overglaze decorating mark in red, crown and oval with initials and "PORCELAINE LIMOGES, FRANCE," ca. 1920s.

Lazeyras, Rosenfeld, and Lehman, Mark 3, overglaze decorating Mark in gray or green, crown with initials, ca. 1920s.

Lazeyras, Rosenfeld, and Lehman, Mark 4, overglaze decorating Mark in blue, "L. R." over "L" with "FRANCE," ca. after 1922.

Lazeyras, Rosenfeld, and Lehman, Mark 5, overglaze decorating Mark in blue, "L. R." with "LIMOGES, FRANCE," ca. after 1922.

L. B. H., overglaze decorating Mark in red, unidentified studio, ca. 1890s.

Legrand, underglaze white ware Mark in green, star between two crescent shapes with "LIMOGES, FRANCE," ca. 1920s.

Leonard, P. H., overglaze exporting Mark in red, blue, or gray, ca. 1890s-1914.

Levy (Imperial), overglaze decorating Mark in red, ca. late 1800s to early 1900s.

Limoges Art Porcelaine, overglaze decorating Mark in green, ca. early 1900s.

Limoges, France (Unidentified Companies), Mark 1, underglaze white ware Mark in green, star in circle, ca. after 1891.

Limoges, France, Mark 2, underglaze white ware Mark in green, "LIMOGES, FRANCE," ca. after 1891.

Limoges, France, Mark 3, underglaze white ware Mark in green, banner, ca. after 1891.

Limoges, France, Mark 4, underglaze white ware Mark in green, crescent, ca. after 1891.

Limoges, France, Mark 5, underglaze white ware Mark in green, "LIMOGES" printed in crescent form over "FRANCE," ca. after 1891.

Limoges, France, Mark 6, underglaze white ware Mark in green, "LIMOGES" printed over "FRANCE," ca. after 1891.

Limoges, France Mark 7, underglaze white ware Mark in green, bird with banner, ca. after 1891.

Limoges, France, Mark 8, overglaze decorating Mark in blue, ca. after 1891.

Limoges, France, Mark 9, overglaze decorating Mark in gray, bees and hive, ca. after 1908.

Maas, S., overglaze Mark in red or blue, ca. 1890s.

Martin, Charles, Mark 1, underglaze white ware Mark in green, bird flying between banners with "LIMOGES, FRANCE," ca. after 1891.

Martin, Charles, Mark 2, underglaze white ware Mark in green, "CM" monogram in triangle, probably used after Mark 1, ca. early 1900s to mid 1930s.

Martin, Charles, Mark 3, overglaze decorating Mark in blue or green, "CM" monogram in triangle with "LIMOGES, FRANCE," and either "DÉCOR," or "DÉPOSÉ," ca. early 1900s to mid 1930s.

Mavaleix, P. M., underglaze white ware Mark in green, "PM DE M" monogram with "LIMOGES, FRANCE," ca. 1908-1914.

MC. D. & S., J., Mark 1, overglaze exporting Mark in red, initials written in script form in oval shape, ca. 1880s-1890.

MC. D. & S., J., Mark 2, overglaze exporting Mark in dark red, crown with initials and "Limoges," ca. after 1890-1914.

Merlin-Lemas, P. (PML) Mark 1, underglaze white ware Mark in green, ca. 1920s.

Merlin-Lemas, P., Mark 2, overglaze decorating Mark in red, "CHATEAU DES P M LEMAS," ca. 1920s.

M. F. & Co., overglaze importing Mark in red for Marshall Field & Co., ca. early 1900s.

Pairpoint, overglaze decorating Mark in green for American decorating company, ca. 1880s.

Paroutaud Frères, Mark 1, underglaze white ware Mark in green, initials with "LA SEYNIE," ca. 1903-1917.

Paroutaud Frères, Mark 2, underglaze white ware Mark in green, "P and P," ca. 1903-1917.

Pastaud, P., overglaze Mark in gold with "peinture fait main" (painted by hand) overglaze in blue-green, ca. 1930s.

Pillivuyt, A., Mark, ca. 1920s.

Plainemaison, underglaze white ware Mark in green, three stars with "LIMOGES, FRANCE," ca. 1890s-1910.

Pouyat, Jean (JP), Mark 1, underglaze white ware Mark in green, initials only, ca. 1850s-1875.

Pouyat, Jean, Mark 2, overglaze decorating Mark in red, initials only, ca. 1850s-1875.

Pouyat, Jean, Mark 3, underglaze white ware Mark in green, initials with line (similar to Mark 1), ca. after 1876-1890.

Pouyat, Jean, Mark 4, overglaze decorating Mark in red, initials with line (similar to Mark 2), ca. 1876-1890.

Pouyat, Jean, Mark 5, underglaze white ware Mark in green with "FRANCE," ca. 1891-1932.

Pouyat, Jean, Mark 6, overglaze decorating Mark in red, similar to Mark 4 but with "FRANCE," ca. after 1890, probably used for a short time.

Pouyat, Jean, Mark 7, overglaze decorating Mark in red, name in circle with "LIMOGES," ca. 1890s-1914.

Pouyat, Jean, Mark 8, overglaze decorating Mark in green, wreath with name, ca. after 1914-1932.

Pouyat, Jean, Mark 9, overglaze decorating Mark in green and pink, wreath with ribbon and name, ca. after 1914-1932.

Raynaud, M. (R&Co.), Mark 1, underglaze white ware Mark in green, initials underscored with "LIMOGES, FRANCE," ca. 1920s-1930s.

Raynaud, M. (R&Co.), Mark 2, overglaze decorating Mark in purple, "R & C LIMOGES" over T&V Bell with "FRANCE," ca. 1920s-1930s.

195

Redon, M., Mark 1, underglaze white ware Mark in green without "FRANCE," ca. 1882-1890.

Redon, M., Mark 2, underglaze white ware Mark in green with "FRANCE," ca. 1891-1896.

Redon, M., Mark 3, overglaze decorating Mark in red or blue, sometimes accompanied by "Special" in a rectangle, in red, ca. 1882-1896.

Redon, M., Mark 4, overglaze decorating Mark in red, name written in script form with "HAND PAINTED," ca. 1882-1896.

Royal China, overglaze decorating Mark in red, ca. after 1922.

Sazerat, L., Mark 1, underglaze white ware Mark in green with "FRANCE," ca. after 1891-late 1890s. The same mark without "FRANCE," ca. before 1891.

Sazerat, L., Mark 2, overglaze decorating Mark in red, name printed inside double circle with a star in the middle, ca. before 1891.

Sazerat, L., Mark 3, overglaze decorating Mark in red with "BLONDEAU, PICHONNIER, and DUBOUCHERON," ca. after 1891-late 1890s.

Serpaut, Charles, underglaze white ware Mark in green, ca. 1920s-1930s.

Straus, Lewis and Sons (LS&S), overglaze exporting Mark in blue, red, green, or gray, ca. 1890s-mid 1920s.

SW, overglaze decorating Mark in red with "BIARRITZ" above wreath with "SW" monogram, ca. after 1891.

Teissonnière, Jules, Mark 1, initials in center of double circle with "PORCELAINES D'ART" printed inside circle, ca. 1908-1940s.

Teissonnière, Jules, Mark 2, initials in shield, "PORCELAINES D'ART," "MADE IN LIMOGES FRANCE," ca. 1908-1940s.

Téxeraud, Léon, Mark 1, "EL TE" over "LIMOGES, FRANCE, UNIQUE," ca. 1920s.

Téxeraud, Léon, Mark 2, "L. T." over "LIMOGES, FRANCE," ca. 1920s.

Tharaud, C., Mark 1, "CT" monogram, ca. 1920s.

196

Tharaud, Mark 2, "C THARAUD" printed in monogram form, ca. 1920s.

Touze, Lemaître Frères, & Blancher, underglaze white ware Mark in green, initials over chicken with "LIMOGES," ca. 1920s.

Tressemann & Vogt (T&V), Mark 1, overglaze exporting Mark in blue, ca. early 1880s-1891.

Tressemann & Vogt, Mark 2, overglaze decorating Mark in purple, red, or gold, bell without "FRANCE," ca. early 1880s.

Tressemann & Vogt, Mark 3, overglaze decorating Mark in brown, rose with "FRANCE," ca. after 1891 (rarely seen).

Tressemann & Vogt Mark, 4a, underglaze white ware Mark in green, initials without "LIMOGES," ca. early 1890s.

Tressemann & Vogt, Mark 4b, underglaze white ware Mark in green, initials with "LIMOGES," ca. 1892-1907, but probably before Mark 5a.

Tressemann & Vogt, Mark 5a, underglaze white ware Mark in green, initials with "FRANCE," ca. 1892-1907.

Tressemann & Vogt, Mark 5b, underglaze white ware Mark in green, like Mark 5a except with "SOUVENIR." This particular mark is found on items decorated with famous people or commemorative events.

Tressemann & Vogt, Mark 6, underglaze white ware Mark in green, initials with "FRANCE, DÉPOSÉ," ca. 1892-1907, probably about 1900.

Tressemann & Vogt, Mark 7, underglaze white ware Mark in green, initials with "LIMOGES, FRANCE," ca. 1892-1907, probably latter part of period.

Tressemann & Vogt, Mark 8, underglaze white ware Mark in green, initials with "LIMOGES, FRANCE, DÉPOSÉ, ca. 1907-1919.

Tressemann & Vogt, Mark 9, overglaze decorating Mark in purple, bell with "FRANCE," ca. 1892-1907, early part of period.

Tressemann & Vogt, Mark 10, overglaze decorating Mark in red or gold, bell with "LIMOGES," ca. 1892-1907, probably about 1900.

Tressemann & Vogt, Mark 11, overglaze decorating Mark in red, brown, or gold, bell with "FRANCE," ca. 1892-1907, latter part of period.

Tressemann & Vogt, Mark 12, overglaze decorating Mark in purple with "FRENCH CHINA" over initials and "LIMOGES," ca. 1907-1919, rarely seen.

Tressemann & Vogt, Mark 13, overglaze decorating Mark in red, "CHINA" over initials with "FRANCE," ca. 1907-1919, rarely seen.

Tressemann & Vogt, Mark 14, overglaze decorating Mark in green with bell and "FRENCH CHINA" printed in banner below, ca. 1907-1919, rarely seen.

Tressemann & Vogt, Mark 15, overglaze decorating Mark in purple, "HAND PAINTED" printed inside double circle around bell.

Tressemann & Vogt, Mark 16, overglaze decorating Mark in purple with "LIMOGES" printed above bell, ca. 1907-1919.

Union Céramique (UC), Mark 1, underglaze white ware Mark in green, ca. 1909-1938.

Union Céramique (UC), Mark 2, overglaze decorating Mark in red, ca. 1909-1938.

Union Limousine, underglaze white ware Mark in green, ca. 1930-1950s.

V. F., underglaze white ware Mark in green, unidentified factory, ca. early 1890s.

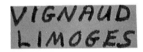

Vignaud Frères, Mark 1, underglaze white ware Mark in green, ca. after 1911-1938.

Vignaud Frères, Mark 2, overglaze decorating Mark in green, fancy "V" with vine and "LIMOGES," ca. 1911-1938.

Vignaud Frères, Mark 3, underglaze white ware Mark in green, "FRANCE, VIGNAUD, LIMOGES," ca. 1938 and after.

Villegoureix, letter "V" in fancy shield, ca. 1920s.

Vultury Frères, underglaze white ware Mark in green, ca. 1887-1904.

Wanamaker's, overglaze importing Mark in green, ca. early 1900s.

Appendix

Six sets of illustrations from several Limoges companies' advertisements dating from the late 1800s and early 1900s are shown here and on the following pages.

1. Several pictures from an undated Ch. Field Haviland brochure feature the mold "Brittany" along with a few others. Notice that only a number indicates the type of decoration. The descriptions of the pieces and their uses show how the china was advertised in the late 1890s. While there is no date indicated, other information in the booklet places its publication circa 1897 or 1898.

2. Some pages from the book *Limoges, It's People, It's China* printed in 1900 for the Bawo & Dotter (Elite Works) factory give descriptions of various shapes or molds, decoration, and even prices.

3. Two advertisements for GDA china (Gérard, Dufraisseix, and Abbot), distributed by Haviland and Abbot in New York were printed in 1904 (butter dish and sandwich set) and 1914 (cup and saucer).

4. Pouyat china, distributed by Paroutaud and Watson in New York is featured in three adverisements published in 1906. Reasons are listed for choosing Pouyat china as "Art-Porcelains."

5. Two pages from different sources advertise blanks and equipment for amateur American china painters. The one including the Charles Field Haviland ad is circa 1897 or 1898, and the other is from a catalog dated November 1901.

6. A pamphlet entitled *Porcelaine Theodore Haviland* and published in August 1912 shows several views of the factory, its workers, and various stages of china production. A few of those pages have been reprinted showing the modeling of pieces, the blanks, and the decorated ware before it was exported.

1. Charles Field Haviland

CH. FIELD HAVILAND

LIMOGES CHINA.

OYSTER PLATE, "WAVE."

This shape with decoration in varied shades
of clouded gold is very rich.

———

Made also for three or four Oysters.

———

Every importer of French China can show you
a large assortment of decors. in
the "C. F. H." ware.

TEA "BRITTANY."
Decor. "450 Bis."

CASSEROLE "BRITTANY"
Decor. "450 Bis."

CH. FIELD HAVILAND

LIMOGES CHINA.

GAME DISH, "BRITTANY."

A game set comprises: 1 Game Dish, 12 Plates
2 Small Dishes for Jelly.

———

A handsome present and useful service.

CH. FIELD HAVILAND

LIMOGES CHINA.

CHOP DISH, "BRITTANY."
Decor. 9749 Frotte.

Just the thing for:—Chops, Game Birds,
Fancy Salads, Strawberry Short Cake,
Moulds of Ice Cream, Etc.

1. Charles Field Haviland

CH. FIELD HAVILAND

LIMOGES CHINA.

RECEPTION PLATE, "BRITTANY."

Something new and good.

———

For use at afternoon parties, five o'clock teas and evening receptions. Convenient and useful for serving Ice Cream and Cake, Salad and Rolls, Fruit, Etc.

CH. FIELD HAVILAND

LIMOGES CHINA.

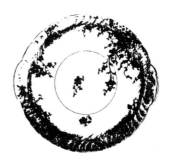

CAKE OR ROLL PLATE, "NORMANDY."

Very useful for a thousand and one purposes.

CH. FIELD HAVILAND

LIMOGES CHINA.

BROTH BOWL, LOUIS XV.

TEAPOT NORMANDY.
Decor. "144 Bis."

2. Bawo & Dotter (Elite Works)

The "Odette" shape is a plain design relieved by a slight rococo edging which admits of exquisite gold tracing and in the absence of tracing gives the pieces a finish which relieves the otherwise smooth surface. The handles are graceful but very strong. The plates and cups and saucers are of egg-shell thinness. The decoration illustrated is an elaborate one. Each piece bears a continuous stipple about the edges in burnished coin gold, interlined with a running floral vine. The decoration proper is a garland of miniature pinks. Such open piece as cups, gravy boats, etc. have garlands of forget-me-nots on the inside. A set of 102 pieces may be obtained of your dealer for about $60.00. Single pieces may be had at any time at the same proportionate cost. Fancy pieces such as Celery Trays, Chop Dishes, etc. to match.

No. 5001.
ODETTE
SHAPE
OPEN
STOCK.

The decoration herewith pictured is one of the best selling ones we ever produced. It was designed specially for the Odette shape and is so laid on the ware that the absence of gold on the edges is not noticeable. It is a wreath of conventionalized violets done in a pleasing purplish color with the stems and leaves in a complementary shading. The elimination of gold on the edges gives the china an appearance of extra thinness. The handles are all stippled with burnished coin gold and the diverging rococo raised work is traced in gold. Like all our open stock patterns this embraces After-Dinner Coffees, Moustache Coffees, Celery Trays, Chop Dishes, etc. Your dealer will furnish a complete set of 102 pieces for about $37.00 or you can buy a dozen plates at the same rate. If he hasn't this particular pattern he will order it for you.

No. 5000.
ODETTE
SHAPE
OPEN
STOCK.

This illustration shows pieces made in the "Perle" shape besides the ones shown in decoration 5002 on a preceding page. Notice the teapot, sugar bowl and cream pitcher—the most beautiful ever made in china. The decoration is a continuous vine of pink and lavender carnations supplemented on the covered ware and inside hollow pieces by an extra vine, similar but of lesser density. The edges of each piece are splashed here and there with burnished coin gold and the handles are carefully traced with gold. This decoration is a very effective one and is nearly one-half less in price than 5002. The ware is exactly the same but there is less detail to the ornamentation. A set of 102 pieces at your dealer's for $54.00.

No. 5000.
PERLE
SHAPE
OPEN
STOCK.

This shape was designed to go with Colonial silver services and to harmonize with dining room furnishings where the whole decorative scheme is after the colonial renaissance which is the vogue of the present day. The sale of it has not been confined to those who have their dining rooms so furnished by any means, because the graceful lines of each piece instantly create enthusiasm in all lovers of artistically formed china. There are sets on this shape in American homes which cost as high as $500.00. A beaded edge is the distinguishing feature of each piece and besides heightening the effect of coin gold, it greatly strengthens the edges of such pieces as plates without making them weighty. The decoration illustrated—festoons of miniature roses with solid burnished gold edges—may be had of any dealer in odd pieces or in sets. A set of 102 pieces may be had of your dealer for about $90.00.

No. 5002
PERLE
SHAPE
OPEN
STOCK.

2. Bawo & Dotter (Elite Works)

The Romeo shape which forms the basis for pattern No. 3004 is one that is exceedingly popular. It is a rococo design with quite a wide bas-relief in the ware on all pieces. The decorative treatment is a border of daisies in the most delicate yellow and green. The effect is a faint greenish one and is very pleasing to the eye. The immense sales testify to its general favor. All handles are stippled with coin gold. Close to the edge a trailing vine takes the place of a gold edge and makes a finish quite as complete. The engraving shows a cake plate and moustache cup—demonstrating the completeness of our open stock patterns. A service of 102 pieces at your dealer's for $37.30. Fancy pieces extra in proportion.

No. 3004, ROMEO SHAPE OPEN STOCK.

The "Marquis" shape is one of the most recent things from the Elite Works. The distinguishing feature is the convex fluting faintly discernable on each piece. With a narrow border in color and supplemented with lace borders in coin gold it is one of the handsomest things ever brought out in china. It is also effective as shown in the engraving. This is a stock pattern with sprays of hawthorn done in pink with leaves in light green. The handles are stippled with coin gold. By the way the handles are very graceful and give an appearance of extra lightness to the covered ware. A set of 102 pieces figures $37.30 and your dealer will supply you at that rate. Separate pieces at the same rate. As in all our open stock patterns the customer has the choice of the old style soup plates with rims or the new coupe shape with no rim. The latter seem to have the call just now.

No. 6076, MARQUIS SHAPE OPEN STOCK.

The variety of Fancy Pieces made at the Elite Works is well-nigh endless. There are shapes aplenty and decorations galore—from the lowest price that good workmanship permits to the very choicest specimens of the modeler's and decorator's art. These include Manicure Trays, Chocolate Pots, Biscuit Jars, Tankards, Chop Dishes, etc. They cost no more than ordinary French china and each bears that guarantee of excellence—the "Elite" trade-mark—when selecting a bit for a gift or for own use. Insist on a piece with the mark. The mark adds naught to the cost. It is a certificate of perfectness.

FANCY PIECES.

There is a greater demand for cups and saucers than for any other single item made in china, with the exception of perhaps those other most necessary articles—plates. So many cups and saucers are bought for presentation purposes; and the fad for "odd" cups and saucers which calls for dozens of cups and saucers no two alike, has greatly argumented the demand. We make a specialty of these goods and in the retail stores you will find hundreds of them in different shapes and decorations selling at from 50c. up. The ones shown in the engraving sell for $1.00 each and the decorations are of a high order of artistic excellence. In no other make of French china will you obtain decorations of such character for the price. On the bottom of the cup or saucer is the tell-tale mark of superiority—the "Elite" stamp. There is no other mark like it on French china—you can't mistake it.

SINGLE CUPS AND SAUCERS.

2. Bawo & Dotter (Elite Works)

There is a distinctiveness about Fish and Game Services coming from the Elite Works that takes them out of the ordinary. The decorative treatment of fish and game subjects by our artists. are not suggested by the time worn studies that have done duty at Limoges for years. There is an originality about Elite conceptions of these subjects just as there is originality in shapes and other decorative treatments that first see the light of day at the Elite Works. You will find very nice ones in the retail shops as low as $12.00 a set and from that up to $100.00. The ware is just as fine quality in the cheaper ones as in the high-cost sets—the elaborateness of the ornamentation only adds to the cost.

FISH AND GAME SETS.

FINE ÉNTREE PLATES.

If one thing had to be singled out from our many productions at the Elite Works as the thing of which we are most proud. we would say it is our line of Fancy Plates. The decorations are laid on many shapes but the " Perle " plate with its beaded edges gives the widest scope to the designer and artist. We will state without fear of contradiction that not even the famous English makes of Coalport. Cauldon. Doulton. Wedgwood. Mintons. etc., can boast of more exquisite designs or more effective colorings. You will find " Elite " plates in the finest retail shops in the country. Elaborateness of design, quality of execution and a lower price, make the " Elite " specimens stand out pre-eminently.

3. Gérard, Dufraisseix, and Abbot (GDA)

4. Jean Pouyat

Pouyat China

has gained a name for superior excellence which is as enduring as

Pouyat China

is durable

You will always know it by these marks

ON DECORATED   ON WHITE

Write for handsome booklet, "Porcelain"

PAROUTAUD & WATSON

SOLE AGENTS

37-39 Murray Street   NEW YORK

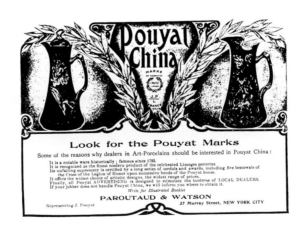

5. Equipment for American China Painters

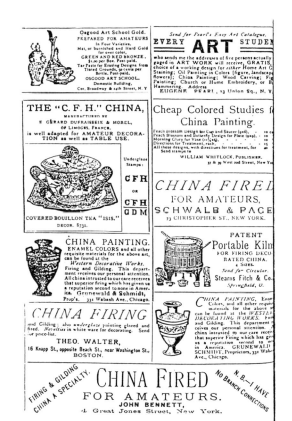

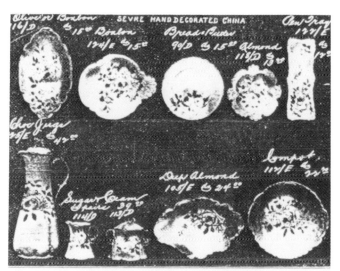

AMERICAN HAND-DECORATED LIMOGES CHINA.

6. Theodore Haviland

6. Theodore Haviland

6. Theodore Haviland

6. Theodore Haviland

Bibliography

d'Albis, Jean and Céleste Romanet. *La Porcelaine de Limoges*. Paris: Editions Sous le Vent, 1980.

Alfassa, Paul et Jacques Guérin. *Porcelaine Française Du XVIIᵉ Au Milieu Du XIXᵉ Siècle*. Paris: Aux Editions Albert Levy, 1931.

Auscher, E. S. *Comment Reconnaitre Les Porcelaines et Les Faiences*. Paris: Librairie Garnier Press, 1914.

———. *A History and Description of French Porcelain*. Translated and edited by William Burton, F.C.S. London: Cassell and Company, Limited, 1905.

Barber, Edwin Atlee. *The Ceramic Collector's Glossary*. New York: The Walpole Society, 1914.

Blanc, Edmond. *Visite D'Une Fabrique De Porcelaine*. Paris: Imprimerie Charles-Lavauzelle & Cie, 1944.

Boger, Louise Ade. *The Dictionary of World Pottery and Porcelain*. New York: Charles Scribner's Sons, 1971.

Brelingard, Desire. *Histoire Du Limousine*. Paris: Presses Universitaires De France, 1950.

Brunhammer, Yvonne, et. al. *Art Nouveau Belgium France: Catalog of an Exhibition Organized by the Institute for the Arts, Rice University, and the Art Institute of Chicago*. Rice University: Institute For the Arts, 1976.

Céramique Impressionniste: L'Atelier Haviland De Paris-Auteuil 1873-1882. Paris: Ancien Hotel Des Archevéques De Sens; Décembre 1974, Février 1975.

Chaffers, William. *Handbook of Marks and Monograms on Pottery and Porcelain*. Revised Edition. London: William Reeves, 1968.

———. *Marks & Monograms on Pottery and Porcelain*. Vol. 1. 15th Revised Edition. London: William Reeves, 1965.

Charles, Bernard H. *Pottery and Porcelain A Dictionary of Terms*. London-Vancouver: David & Charles, 1974.

Clark, Eleanor. *Plate Collecting*. Secaucus, New Jersey: Citadel Press, 1976.

Collard, Elizabeth. *Nineteenth-Century Pottery and Porcelain in Canada*. Montreal: McGill University Press, 1967.

Cox, W. E. *The Book of Pottery and Porcelain*. Vol. 1. New York: L. Lee Shepard Co., Inc., 1944.

Cushion, John Patrick (in collaboration with W. B. Honey). *Handbook of Pottery and Porcelain Marks*. London: Faber & Faber, 1956.

———. *Pocketbook of French and Italian Ceramic Marks*. London: Faber & Faber, 1965.

Danckert, Ludwig. *Handbuch des Europäischen Porzellans*. Munchen: Prestel-Verlag, 1954.

Eberlein, Harold Donaldson and Roger Wearne Ramsdell. *The Practical Book of Chinaware*. Philadelphia and New York: J. B. Lippincott Company, 1925 and 1948.

Ernould-Gandouet, Marielle. *La Céramique en France au XIXᵉ Siècle*. Paris: Gründ, 1969.

Fontaine, Georges. *La Ceramique Française*. Paris: Presses Universitaires De France, 1965.

Gaston, Mary Frank. *The Collector's Encyclopedia of Limoges Porcelain*. Paducah, Kentucky: Collector Books, 1980; Revised Prices, 1984.

———. *Haviland Collectables and Objects of Art*. Paducah, Kentucky: Collector Books, 1984.

———. "Limoges Porcelain: French and American Decoration." *The Antique Trader Weekly*, July 3, 1985.

———. "Limoges Porcelain." *The Antique Trader Price Guide To Antiques*, April, 1986.

Gérard, Dufraisseix & Cie. Catalog. *The Ch. Field Haviland Limoges China*, n. d. (circa 1890s).

Grollier, Charles de. *Manuel de L'Amateur De Porcelaines*. Paris: Auguste Piccard Ed., 1922.

Haggar, Reginald G. *The Concise Encyclopedia of Continental Pottery and Porcelain*. New York: Hawthorne Books, Inc., 1960.

Hamer, Frank. *The Potter's Dictionary of Materials and Techniques*. London: Pitman Publishing; New York: Watson-Guptill Publications, 1975.

Head, Margaret G. *Charles Field Haviland China Identification Guide*, Book 1. Monroe, Michigan: E. C. Kraus Printing, 1982.

Hillier, Bevis. *Pottery and Porcelain 1700-1914*. New York: Meredith Press, 1968.

Honey, W. B. *European Ceramic Art*. Faber & Faber, 1952.

———. *French Porcelain of the 18th Century*. London: Faber & Faber, 1950.

How Things Work. Vol. II. Geneva: Bibliographisches Institut and Simon and Schuster Inc., American Edition, n. d.

Jamreau, Guillaume. *Les Arts Du Feu.* Paris: Presses Universitaires, 1948.

Jenkins, Dorothy H. *A Fortune in the Junk Pile.* New York: Crown Publishers, Inc., 1963.

Jacobsen, Gertrude Tatnall. *Haviland China: Volume One.* Des Moines, Iowa: Wallace-Homestead, 1979.

Kovel, Ralph M. and Terry H. Kovel. *Dictionary of Marks: Pottery and Porcelain.* New York: Crown Publishers, Inc., 1953 and 1972.

————. *Know Your Antiques.* New York: Crown Publishers. Inc., 1967 and 1973.

————. *Kovel's New Dictionary of Marks.* New York: Crown Publishers, Inc., 1986.

Landais, Hubert. *La Porcelaine Française XVIIIe Siècle.* Paris: La Librairie Hachette, 1963.

Le Duc, Geneviève et Henri Curtil. *Marques Et Signatures De La Porcelaine Française.* Paris: Éditions Charles Massin, 1970.

Les Porcelaines Françaises. Avant-propos de Mm. Marc H. Gobert et M. Leyendecker. Paris: Tardy, 1950.

Lesur, Adrien and Tardy. *Les Porcelaines Françaises.* Paris: Tardy, 1967.

"Limoges ou Deux Siècles de Porcelaine." Pp. 87-103 in *Revue des Industries d'Art Offrir.* August, 1978.

Mackay, James. *Dictionary of Turn of the Century Antiques.* London: Ward Lock Limited, 1974.

O'Gorman, Joseph H. *Limoges – Its People – Its China.* Prepared by the editor of the B. & D. Bulletin. New York: Bawo & Dotter, 1900.

Mésière, Ernest (ed.). *Porcelaine Theodore Haviland.* Paris: Haviland Company, 1912.

Penkala, Maria. *European Porcelain A Handbook for the Collector.* Second Edition. Rutland, Vermont: Charles E. Tuttle, 1968.

Platt, Dorothy Pickard. *The Story of Pickard China.* Hanover, Pennsylvania: Everybody's Press, Inc., 1970.

Poche, Emanuel. *Porcelain Marks of the World.* New York: Arco Publishing Co., Inc., 1974.

Rhodes, Daniel. *Stoneware and Porcelain: The Art of High-Fired Pottery,* Philadelphia: Chilton Company, 1959.

Robert, Maurice. *Les Poteries Populaires Et Les Potiers Du Limousin Et De La Marche (du XVIIIe siècle a nos jours).* Paris: Editions F. E. R. N., 1972.

Röntgen, Robert E. *Marks on German, Bohemian and Austrian Porcelain 1710 to the Present.* Exton, Pennsylvania: Schiffer Publishing Co., 1981.

Rothenberg, Polly. *The Complete Book of Ceramic Art.* New York: Crown Publishers, 1972.

Savage, George. *Ceramics For The Collector An Introduction to Pottery and Porcelain.* New York: The MacMillan Company, 1949.

————. *Seventeenth and Eighteenth Century French Porcelain.* New York: MacMillan Company, 1960.

Savage, George and Harold Neuman. *An Illustrated Dictionary of Ceramics.* New York: Van Nostrand Reinhold Company, 1974.

Schleiger, Arlene. *Two Hundred Patterns of Haviland China,* Books I, II, III, IV. Omaha, Nebraska: Arlene Schleiger, 1973, 1970, 1969, 1968.

Thorn, C. Jordan. *Handbook of Old Pottery & Porcelain Marks.* New York: Tudor Publishing Company, 1947.

Tilmans, Emile. *Porcelaines De France.* Paris: Editions Mondes, 1953.

Van Patten, Joan F. *The Collector's Encyclopedia of Nippon Porcelain.* Paducah, Kentucky: Collector Books, 1979.

Weiss, Gustav. *Book of Porcelain.* Translated by Janet Seligman. New York: Praeger Publishers, Inc., 1971.

Wood, Serry. *Haviland, Limoges.* Watkins-Glen, New York: Century House, 1951.

Wynter, Harriet. *An Introduction to European Porcelain.* London: Arlington Books, 1971.

Young, Harriet. *Grandmother's Haviland.* Second Revised Edition. Des Moines, Iowa: Wallace-Homestead Book Co., 1970.

Index To Objects

(by Photograph Numbers)

Index And Cross Reference To Companies, Initials, And Symbols

This index is arranged alphabetically and corresponds to the listing of factories and studios following the photographs and to the marks following those companies. Refer to these sections on companies and marks, which are arranged alphabetically, for information. The numbers in this index refer only to the photograph numbers. Not every name, initial, or symbol listed in this index has an example pictured, but there is information on each entry either in the list of companies or in the section on marks, but no page numbers are shown. For example, "Ardant, H." is listed in the index without any number beside the name. Thus, there is not a picture shown for Ardant's production, but he is listed alphabetically in the list of companies, and his mark is shown, again in alphabetical order under his name, in the section on marks.

Index To French Artists' Signatures

Index To Professional American Decorators

Price Guide

Plate 1 ....$1,000.00–1,200.00
Plate 2 ....$1,200.00–1,400.00
Plate 3 ....$1,200.00–1,400.00
Plate 4 ....$4,000.00–5,000.00
Plate 5 ....$350.00–400.00
Plate 6 ....$350.00–400.00
Plate 7 ....$350.00–400.00
Plate 8 ....$1,200.00–1,400.00
Plate 9 ....$800.00–1,000.00
Plate 10 ....$600.00–700.00
Plate 11 ....$700.00–800.00
Plate 12 ....$1,300.00–1,500.00
Plate 13 ....$3,000.00–3,500.00
Plate 14 ....$2,500.00–3,000.00
Plate 15 ....$375.00–425.00
Plate 16 ....(see Plate 15)
Plate 17 ....$800.00–1,000.00
Plate 18 ....$450.00–550.00
Plate 19 ....$800.00–900.00
Plate 20 ....(see Plate 19)
Plate 21 ....$800.00–1,000.00
Plate 22 ....$1,800.00–2,000.00
Plate 23 ....$2,800.00–3,000.00
Plate 24 ....$1,200.00–1,400.00
Plate 25 ....$2,300.00–2,500.00
Plate 26 ....$1,400.00–1,600.00
Plate 27 ....(see Plate 26)
Plate 28 ....$6,500.00–6,800.00
Plate 29 ....(see Plate 28)
Plate 30 ....$550.00–650.00
Plate 31 ....$800.00–1,000.00
Plate 32 ....$400.00–475.00
Plate 33 ....$1,200.00–1,400.00
Plate 34 ....$1,200.00–1,400.00
Plate 35 ....$1,000.00–1,200.00
Plate 36 ....$250.00–300.00
Plate 37 ....$200.00–250.00
Plate 38 ....$575.00–675.00
Plate 39 ....$575.00–675.00
Plate 40 ....$300.00–350.00
Plate 41 ....$375.00–425.00
Plate 42 ....$250.00–300.00
Plate 43 ....$300.00–350.00
Plate 44 ....$250.00–300.00
Plate 45 ....$325.00–375.00
Plate 46 ....$250.00–300.00
Plate 47 ....$300.00–350.00
Plate 48 ....$375.00–425.00
Plate 49 ....$325.00–375.00
Plate 50 ....$550.00–650.00
Plate 51 ....$475.00–525.00

Plate 52 ....$475.00–525.00
Plate 53 ....$1,400.00–1,600.00
Plate 54 ....$300.00–350.00
Plate 55 ....$550.00–650.00
Plate 56 ....$375.00–425.00
Plate 57 ....$500.00–550.00
Plate 58 ....$500.00–550.00
Plate 59 ....$425.00–475.00
Plate 60 ....$375.00–425.00
Plate 61 ....$300.00–350.00
Plate 62 ....$200.00–250.00
Plate 63 ....$650.00–750.00 set
Plate 64 ....$300.00–350.00
Plate 65 ....$325.00–375.00
Plate 66 ....$275.00–325.00
Plate 67 ....$275.00–325.00
Plate 68 ....$275.00–325.00
Plate 69 ....$225.00–275.00
Plate 70 ....$300.00–350.00
Plate 71 ....$175.00–200.00
Plate 72 ....$55.00–65.00
Plate 73 ....$75.00–100.00
Plate 74 ....$160.00 180.00
Plate 75 ....$140.00–160.00
Plate 76 ....$160.00–180.00
Plate 77 ....$40.00–50.00
Plate 78 ....$45.00–55.00
Plate 79 ....$150.00–175.00 set
Plate 80 ....$250.00–300.00 set
Plate 81 ....$175.00–200.00
Plate 82 ....$250.00–300.00
Plate 83 ....$450.00–500.00
Plate 84 ....$450.00–500.00
Plate 85 ....$200.00–250.00
Plate 86 ....$400.00–450.00
Plate 87 ....$275.00–325.00
Plate 88 ....$250.00–300.00
Plate 89 ....$400.00–450.00
Plate 90 ....$300.00–350.00
Plate 91 ....$550.00–650.00
Plate 92 ....$1,000.00–1,200.00 set
Plate 93 ....$220.00–240.00
Plate 94 ....$150.00–175.00
Plate 95 ....$175.00–200.00
Plate 96 ....$350.00–400.00
Plate 97 ....$2,600.00–2,800.00 set
Plate 98 ....$750.00–850.00
Plate 99 ....$2,200.00–2,400.00 set
Plate 100 ....(see Plate 99)
Plate 101 ....$2,400.00–2,600.00 set
Plate 102 ....(see Plate 101)
Plate 103 ....$2,000.00–2,200.00 set
Plate 104 ....$200.00–225.00 set
Plate 105 ....$1,400.00–1,600.00 set
Plate 106 ....$150.00–175.00
Plate 107 ....$220.00–240.00 each
Plate 108 ....$200.00–235.00

Plate 220	$300.00–325.00
Plate 221	$500.00–600.00
Plate 222	$500.00–600.00
Plate 223	$400.00–500.00
Plate 224	$225.00–275.00
Plate 225	$1,000.00–1,200.00 set
Plate 226	$200.00–225.00 pair
Plate 227	$275.00–325.00
Plate 228	$150.00–175.00
Plate 229	$300.00–350.00
Plate 230	$150.00–175.00
Plate 231	$350.00–400.00 set
Plate 232	$80.00–100.00
Plate 233	$225.00–250.00
Plate 234	$140.00–160.00
Plate 235	$125.00–150.00
Plate 236	$125.00–150.00
Plate 237	$125.00–150.00
Plate 238	$225.00–250.00
Plate 239	$90.00–110.00
Plate 240	$90.00–110.00
Plate 241	$80.00–100.00
Plate 242	$100.00–125.00
Plate 243	$200.00–225.00
Plate 244	$150.00–175.00
Plate 245	$130.00–150.00
Plate 246	$130.00–150.00
Plate 247	$150.00–175.00
Plate 248	$150.00–175.00
Plate 249	$160.00–180.00
Plate 250	$170.00–190.00
Plate 251	$110.00–130.00
Plate 252	$110.00–130.00
Plate 253	$110.00–130.00
Plate 254	$125.00–150.00
Plate 255	$110.00–130.00
Plate 256	$125.00–150.00
Plate 257	$275.00–300.00
Plate 258	$120.00–140.00
Plate 259	$250.00–275.00
Plate 260	$250.00–300.00
Plate 261	$300.00–350.00
Plate 262	$250.00–300.00
Plate 263	$200.00–250.00
Plate 264	$300.00–350.00
Plate 265	$300.00–350.00
Plate 266	$70.00–80.00
Plate 267	$80.00–90.00 mug
	$150.00–175.00 covered bouillon cup
Plate 268	$70.00–80.00
Plate 269	$55.00–65.00
Plate 270	$45.00–55.00 (mc)
Plate 271	$150.00–170.00
Plate 272	$40.00–50.00
Plate 273	$45.00–55.00
Plate 274	$70.00–80.00
Plate 275	$275.00–325.00

Plate 276	$60.00–75.00
Plate 277	$65.00–75.00
Plate 278	$35.00–40.00
Plate 279	$35.00–40.00
Plate 280	$15.00–18.00
Plate 281	$35.00–40.00
Plate 282	$15.00–18.00
Plate 283	$275.00–300.00
Plate 284	$15.00–18.00
Plate 285	$175.00–200.00 set
Plate 286	$175.00–200.00 set
Plate 287	$75.00–85.00
Plate 288	$45.00–55.00
Plate 289	$75.00–85.00
Plate 290	$50.00–60.00
Plate 291	$100.00–120.00
Plate 292	$300.00–325.00
Plate 293	$80.00–100.00
Plate 294	$275.00–325.00
Plate 295	$300.00–350.00
Plate 296	$240.00–260.00
Plate 297	$15.00–18.00
Plate 298	$30.00–35.00
Plate 299	$375.00–425.00
Plate 300	$25.00–35.00
Plate 301	$140.00–160.00
Plate 302	$75.00–85.00
Plate 303	$120.00–140.00
Plate 304	$150.00–175.00
Plate 305	$150.00–175.00
Plate 306a	$300.00–350.00 set
Plate 306b	$125.00–150.00
Plate 307	$1,600.00–1,800.00 set
Plate 308	$125.00–150.00
Plate 309	$150.00–175.00
Plate 310	$225.00–275.00
Plate 311	$150.00–175.00
Plate 312	$125.00–150.00
Plate 313	$40.00–50.00
Plate 314	$165.00–185.00
Plate 315	$80.00–90.00
Plate 316	$150.00–175.00
Plate 317	$150.00–175.00
Plate 318	$600.00–700.00 set
Plate 319	$400.00–500.00
Plate 320	$400.00–450.00 set
Plate 321	(see Plate 320)
Plate 322	(see Plate 320)
Plate 323	$325.00–375.00 set
Plate 324	$175.00–200.00
Plate 325	$425.00–475.00
Plate 326	$200.00–225.00
Plate 327	$60.00–70.00
Plate 328	$150.00–175.00
Plate 329	$70.00–80.00
Plate 330	$165.00–185.00
Plate 331	$750.00–850.00

Plate 332 ....$1,200.00–1,300.00
Plate 333 ....$1,500.00–1,700.00
Plate 334 ....$300.00–325.00
Plate 335 ....$80.00–100.00
Plate 336 ....$450.00–500.00 set
Plate 337 ....$175.00–225.00
Plate 338 ....$14.00–18.00
Plate 339 ....$75.00–85.00
Plate 340a $375.00–425.00
Plate 340b $150.00–175.00
Plate 341 ....$375.00–425.00 set
Plate 342 ....$1,600.00–1,800.00
Plate 343 ....$2,400.00–2,600.00
Plate 344 ....$2,600.00–2,800.00
Plate 345 ....$3,000.00–3,200.00
Plate 346 ....$2,800.00–3,000.00
Plate 347 ....$2,800.00–3,000.00
Plate 348 ....$700.00–800.00
Plate 349 ....$1,600.00–1,800.00
Plate 350 ....$300.00–325.00
Plate 351 ....$275.00–300.00
Plate 352 ....$300.00–325.00
Plate 353 ....$200.00–225.00
Plate 354 ....$325.00–375.00
Plate 355 ....$350.00–400.00
Plate 356 ....$125.00–150.00
Plate 357 ....$120.00–140.00
Plate 358 ....$150.00–175.00
Plate 359 ....$300.00–325.00 set
Plate 360 ....$400.00–450.00 set
Plate 361 ....$70.00–80.00
Plate 362 ....$45.00–55.00 set
Plate 363 ....$600.00–700.00
Plate 364 ....$500.00–600.00
Plate 365 ....$650.00–750.00
Plate 366 ....$300.00–325.00
Plate 367 ....$375.00–400.00
Plate 368 ....$1,000.00–1,200.00
Plate 369 ....$350.00–375.00
Plate 370 ....$325.00–350.00
Plate 371 ....$550.00–650.00
Plate 372 ....$350.00–400.00
Plate 373 ....$300.00–350.00
Plate 374 ....$550.00–650.00
Plate 375 ....$325.00–375.00
Plate 376 ....$85.00–95.00
Plate 377 ....$80.00–90.00
Plate 378 ....$80.00–90.00
Plate 379 ....$500.00–550.00
Plate 380 ....$325.00–350.00
Plate 381 ....$750.00–850.00
Plate 382 ....$240.00–260.00
Plate 383 ....$240.00–260.00
Plate 384 ....$350.00–375.00
Plate 385 ....$325.00–350.00
Plate 386a $225.00–250.00
Plate 386b $60.00–75.00

Plate 387 ....$75.00–85.00
Plate 388 ....$90.00–110.00
Plate 389 ....$80.00–90.00
Plate 390 ....$75.00–90.00
Plate 391 ....$125.00–150.00
Plate 392 ....$140.00–160.00
Plate 393 ....$150.00–170.00
Plate 394 ....$175.00–200.00
Plate 395 ....$100.00–120.00
Plate 396 ....$130.00–150.00 set
Plate 397 ....$75.00–85.00
Plate 398 ....$125.00–150.00
Plate 399 ....$130.00–150.00
Plate 400 ....$220.00–240.00
Plate 401 ....$90.00–110.00
Plate 402 ....$375.00–425.00
Plate 403 ....$250.00–300.00
Plate 404 ....$200.00–$225.00
Plate 405 ....$150.00–175.00
Plate 406 ....$120.00–130.00
Plate 407 ....$225.00–250.00
Plate 408 ....$300.00–350.00 set
Plate 409 ....$125.00–150.00
Plate 410 ....$375.00–425.00
Plate 411 ....$120.00–140.00
Plate 412 ....$350.00–400.00
Plate 413 ....$225.00–250.00
Plate 414 ....$120.00–140.00
Plate 415 ....$300.00–350.00
Plate 416 ....$275.00–325.00
Plate 417 ....$200.00–240.00
Plate 418 ....$200.00–250.00
Plate 419 ....$200.00–240.00
Plate 420 ....$275.00–325.00
Plate 421 ....$175.00–200.00
Plate 422 ....$275.00–325.00
Plate 423 ....$350.00–400.00
Plate 424 ....$400.00–450.00
Plate 425 ....$250.00–300.00
Plate 426 ....$250.00–300.00
Plate 427 ....$350.00–400.00
Plate 428 ....$300.00–350.00
Plate 429 ....$120.00–140.00
Plate 430 ....$325.00–375.00
Plate 431 ....$350.00–400.00
Plate 432 ....$300.00–350.00
Plate 433 ....$400.00–450.00
Plate 434 ....$450.00–500.00
Plate 435 ....$325.00–350.00
Plate 436 ....$30.00–40.00 each
Plate 437 ....$450.00–500.00
Plate 438 ....$100.00–120.00
Plate 439 ....$300.00–350.00
Plate 440 ....$300.00–350.00
Plate 441 ....$1,000.00–1,200.00 set
Plate 442 ....$400.00–450.00
Plate 443 ....$200.00–225.00

Plate 444 ....$200.00–225.00	Plate 473 ....$40.00–50.00
Plate 445 ....$325.00–375.00	Plate 474 ....$150.00–175.00
Plate 446 ....$350.00–400.00	Plate 475 ....$125.00–150.00
Plate 447 ....$375.00–425.00	Plate 476 ....$150.00–175.00
Plate 448 ....$350.00–400.00	Plate 477 ....$100.00–125.00 set
Plate 449 ....$325.00–375.00	Plate 478 ....$50.00–60.00
Plate 450 ....$375.00–425.00	Plate 479 ....$140.00–160.00 set
Plate 451 ....$225.00–250.00	Plate 480 ....$35.00–45.00
Plate 452 ....$375.00–425.00	Plate 481 ....$60.00–70.00
Plate 453 ....$350.00–400.00	Plate 482 ....$60.00–70.00
Plate 454 ....$150.00–175.00	Plate 483 ....$45.00–55.00
Plate 455 ....$150.00–175.00	Plate 484 ....$100.00–120.00
Plate 456 ....$220.00–240.00	Plate 485 ....$35.00–45.00
Plate 457 ....$200.00–250.00	Plate 486 ....$50.00–60.00
Plate 458 ....$200.00–250.00	Plate 487 ....$80.00–90.00
Plate 459 ....$220.00–240.00 pair	Plate 488 ....$90.00–110.00
Plate 460 ....$150.00–175.00	Plate 489 ....$55.00–65.00
Plate 461 ....$40.00–50.00	Plate 490 ....$65.00–75.00
Plate 462 ....$150.00–175.00	Plate 491 ....$80.00–90.00
Plate 463 ....$275.00–325.00 set	Plate 492 ....$80.00–100.00
Plate 464 ....$325.00–375.00 set	Plate 493 ....$100.00–125.00
Plate 465 ....$30.00–40.00	Plate 494 ....$50.00–60.00 set
Plate 466 ....$50.00–60.00	Plate 495 ....$35.00–45.00 each
Plate 467 ....$30.00–40.00	Plate 496 ....$120.00–140.00
Plate 468 ....$100.00–120.00	Plate 497 ....$200.00–225.00
Plate 469 ....$140.00–160.00	Plate 498 ....$150.00–175.00
Plate 470 ....$140.00–160.00	Plate 499 ....$160.00–185.00
Plate 471 ....$40.00–50.00	Plate 500 ....$125.00–150.00
Plate 472 ....$20.00–25.00 each	

Other Books By Mary Frank Gaston

The Collector's Encyclopedia of R. S. Prussia	$24.95
The Collector's Encyclopedia of R. S. Prussia, Second Series	$24.95
The Collector's Encyclopedia of R. S. Prussia, Third Series	$24.95
The Collector's Encyclopedia of R.S. Prussia, Fourth Series	$24.95
The Collector's Encyclopedia of Flow Blue China, Second Series	$24.95
Blue Willow, Second Edition	$14.95
Art Deco	$14.95

These titles may be ordered from the author or the publisher.
Include $2.00 each for postage and handling.

Mary Frank Gaston
P.O. Box 342
Bryan, TX 77806

Collector Books
P.O. Box 3009
Paducah, KY 42001

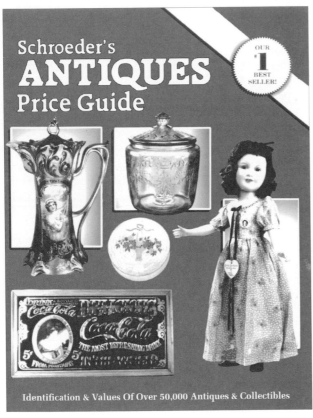